BRING HOME THE BACON

BRING HOME THE BACON

BECOME A PERSUASIVE LEADER WITH THE PROVEN S3P3 SYSTEM

Larry Tracy

Edited by:
Christie Wagner

What Others Say of Larry Tracy's Speaking and Coaching

"You have been a splendid spokesman for America... an extraordinarily effective speaker... meeting with hundreds of audiences at the White House and in communities across the country, as well as abroad. You have, on the platform, radio and TV helped the people hear the facts and debunk the myths concerning Central America."

President Ronald Reagan

"Larry Tracy is the most outstanding Lieutenant Colonel of any service in the Defense Intelligence Agency. No officer has done more to establish this Agency's professionalism than he. Laudatory comments on his briefings from General Officers from throughout the Departent of Defense regularly flow into my office."

Samuel V. Wilson, Lieutenant General, USA
Director, Defense Intelligence Agency

"When I was in charge of The Army Engineer School, I had the students critique the various courses of instruction in order to improve them. Then-Major Tracy's courses in strategic and tactical intelligence always received the highest positive ratings. I observed that he presented his material outstandingly and that he greatly motivated young officers. When it comes to presenting and motivating, Larry Tracy is THE expert."

Ira A. Hunt, Major General, USA (Ret)
Former Commandant, U.S. Army Engineer School

"Colonel Tracy's briefing was among the finest that the Board has ever received. The quality and range of the presentation was superb. He did an outstanding job!"

Louis J. Conti, Chairman, Reserve Forces Policy Board

"In a Department that prides itself on its communication skills, you, an Army colonel, became the standard to match in public oratory."

Ambassador Otto Reich, U.S. Department of State

"I just wanted to express my deep appreciation for the excellent presentation you made at our Law Professor Workshop in Saint Louis. I thought the entire program went extremely well, and I especially enjoyed your contribution."

Robert Turner,
Standing Committee on Law and National Security
American Bar Association

"Your contribution, through your speaking skills, to our understanding of the grave threats to freedom in Central America cannot be understated."

Reprentative Henry J. Hyde,
Member of Congress

"I want to thank you for taking the time to serve as a panelist on the Central America Issues Forum in Brooklyn this past Sunday. You were an excellent speaker and your contributions to fuller understanding of the issues involved were appreciated by all attending."

Representative Charles E. Schumer,
Member of Congress

"Larry Tracy is one of the most articulate advocates I've ever seen operate on the platform. He's crisp and clear, his logic and thinking first-rate. As a speech coach myself, I continue to learn from him"

John Jay Daly, Founder,
National Capital Speakers Association

"I wanted to express a 'heartfelt thanks' for all of your help during our oral boards prep process.... From my perspective, our success was due in no small way to you guiding us along the process. I greatly appreciated the carefully chosen words you provided for my closing remarks. They kept us on point and were powerful words!"

Dan Balberchak Jr. Captain, USN (Ret), Deputy Project Manager
Sayers and Associates, San Diego, CA

"In my years of experience in training and development, I have never read more enthusiastic seminar evaluations. You showed our people how to convert arcane and complex technical information into a clear and persuasive presentation."

Bill Fender, Manager, Human Resources,
LOGICON Operating Systems, Arlington, VA

"Your seminar on "Advocacy" for NASA Program and Project Managers was one of the best I have seen in my professional experience."

Francis Hoban, Manager,
NASA Project Manager Training Initiative

"Larry Tracy's training is based on the real world--the high profile "fishbowls" of the White House, and the national security, intelligence and defense establishments. All are high stakes crucibles where clear and concise communications can make or break decisions, policies, careers, and even administrations. He shows how to deliver your message in the most persuasive manner possible."

Jim McCarthy, Owner, AOC Key Solutions,
Chantilly, VA

"Larry Tracy's speech 'Taming Hostile Audiences' is a model of it kind, an outstanding speech…that teaches a number of invaluable lessons on how to give a winning performance, even to the most hostile of audiences."

**Aram Bakshian, Jr. Editor in Chief,
American Speaker magazine**

"I have been trying cases for over thirty years, and have given a number of legal papers. It was surprising to me how much your training contributed to my presentation ability."

**Carl G. Love, Partner, Cushman, Darby and Cushman,
Attorneys at Law, Washington D.C.**

"I recently used techniques of Larry Tracy to coach the management team on a proposal requiring an oral presentation. The result? A WIN worth over $300 Million to my company. Enough said!

**Keith Wallace, Program Manager,
The Wylie Corporation**

"The ability to get buy-in is one of the most valuable skills that an employee or manager can have to be successful. Larry Tracy is a recognized expert in presentations training. He received the highest evaluations we've ever had."

**Anne Kelly, CEO, Federal Consulting Group,
Department of the Treasury**

"You not only trained twenty-two people how to speak convincingly in some fairly hostile situations, but in two cases your training actually changed personalities."

**Steven Cox, Director, Office of Intelligence and Threat Analysis
U.S. Department of State**

"Yours was certainly one of the liveliest training sessions we have ever held at a Counsel Seminar. You held the attention of 130 attorneys...and imparted solid knowledge on how to construct and give an effective oral presentation. Defense Logistics Agency attorneys will use this knowledge often in advising our clients."

Bruce W. Baird, General Counsel,
Defense Logistics Agency

"Larry, your two presentations at our 'Thought Leadership Conference' in Washington, DC, were exceptional! Attendees are STILL speaking about the practicality of your approach and the methodology you taught us all to use to overcome fear and discomfort when speaking in public."

Charles "Skip" Pettit, President,
International Training Consortium

Preface

You are probably **wondering "Why should I buy this book, what will I gain from it?"**

The short answer: You'll be on the way to acquiring perhaps the most critical skill needed for leadership in the 21st Century-the ability to persuade with words. A great corporate leader in the United States, Jack Welch, former CEO of General Electric, wrote in 2016

> *"...I've come to believe a person's skill in public speaking – be it in front of a crowd of 1,000 strangers or a meeting with five close associates – is more essential than ever. Making your case in writing is increasingly a thing of the past. You are what you say; your communication approach is your fingerprint, both professional and personal."*

There are many excellent books providing examples of famous leaders-Eisenhower, Lincoln, Churchill, etc. Other valuable books show the qualities of a leader. Few, if any, teach a step-by-step method to deliver those persuasive presentations which can make you an influential leader. This book does.

You may be thinking "I know how important persuasive speaking is to be a leader, but I'm petrified at speaking in public." Understandable. Surveys show "public speaking" to be among the top fears in the United

States. In this book I'll show you techniques to make this fear your ally, not your foe.

I'm a retired Army colonel who did more speaking than shooting. In one such assignment I headed the Defense Intelligence Agency's Presentation Branch, responsible for the daily intelligence briefings to the Chairman of the Joint Chiefs of Staff. I facilitated over 500 such briefings, and presented personally to the Chairman almost 100 times. In another, I was detailed by the White House to the State Department to debate controversial issues before critical, often hostile, audiences. Feedback to the White House resulted in President Reagan calling me "An extraordinarily effective speaker."

In these assignments, I used a method I called "The S3P3 System." It had its origin in advice I received from a Sergeant Major when I was a Second Lieutenant. He recommended I use a four-word formula he had developed: *Anticipate, Draft, Practice, Deliver*. I took this advice to heart, as he had been in the Army longer than I had been on earth. It definitely improved my speaking ability, imposing structure and focus on my Irish gift of gab.

Over time, as the presentations I was required to deliver became more complex, that four-word formula morphed into the S3P3 System. Visualize it as the pillars of *Substance, Structure* and *Style* supporting the pyramid of *Planning, Practicing* and *Presenting*. This book will show you how to use this method to deliver presentations to audiences opposed to your position as well as to supportive groups requiring precise information.

After retiring from the Army, I became a speech coach and was cited in the books <u>Information Please Business Almanac and Sourcebook,</u> published by Houghton-Mifflin, <u>Best of the Best</u>, published by Insight Publishing, and <u>What to Say When... You're Dying on the Platform,</u> published by McGraw-Hill. My coaching workshops, are, of course, based on the S3P3 System.

The book cover says the S3P3 System is proven. Given that the word "proven" is often dishonest spin and outright hucksterism, how can I say that? I say it because I developed and used the S3P3 System in challenging speaking situations throughout my career. If it hadn't worked in those assignments, I would have been fired. But it did, and it has worked for participants in my coaching workshops. I am confident it will work for you.

The twenty-one chapters in this book will provide you an easily-learned method to deliver persuasive presentations which enhance your reputation as an influential leader. Moreover, what psychologists refer to as the "Halo Effect" will result in others, such as your boss, valuing you as highly intelligent, very competent, and a "go to" person.

In the Appendices at the end of the book you'll find two articles which show how the S3P3 System can be applied to different speaking challenges. Appendix 1 is a speech turned article showing how to deal with a resistant audience. *Taming Hostile Audiences: Persuading Those Who Would Rather Jeer than Cheer* was originally a presentation I delivered to professional speakers. It was subsequently published in the prestigious <u>Vital Speeches of the Day</u>, and <u>American Speaker,</u> the top magazine on public speaking instruction in the US.

Appendix 2 is an article I wrote for the Project Management Institute of Washington, DC, *Model for a Winning Oral Presentation: The Philly Cheesesteak*. It was well accepted by Project Managers who must lead teams vying for federal contracts as a realistic way to prepare for these grueling experiences and was published in other professioanl newsletters.

Take a look at the next few pages to determine if the S3P3 System can be of help when you must demonstrate your leadership by "bringing home the bacon."

Larry Tracy

About the Author

A GRADUATE OF ST. Joseph's University in Philadelphia, Larry Tracy also earned a Master's degree from Georgetown University followed by post-graduate studies. After he retired from the United States Army as a Colonel he converted his global speaking experience into a career as a speech coach and has been cited in many publications as one of the top such coaches in the United States.

During the Cold War he served as the senior intelligence briefer to the Chairman of the Joint Chiefs of Staff. The White House later assigned him to the State Department to defend and debate controversial policies throughout the United States.

He served in Vietnam, Argentina and Bolivia, speaks fluent Spanish and has conducted presentation skills workshops in that language.

Larry's military education includes the U.S. Army Command and General Staff College at Fort Leavenworth, Kansas and the Inter-American Defense College at Fort McNair in Washington, DC.

Dedication
To My Wife Fely

SHE HAS BEEN the driving force behind this book. She knew I was happier in front of an audience than behind a computer and constantly encouraged and cajoled me to sit and write. She believed I should share my speaking experience with a wider audience than I could ever reach by speaking. I am so very grateful to her for pushing me to write, not just speak. This book would not have been written without her. Thanks, Fel.

CONTENTS

Introduction

THE PREFACE EXPLAINED how I came to the field of speech coaching, and how my S3P3 System evolved. In this Introduction I want to discuss the core of this book, the 21 chapters showing how to Plan, Practice and Present.

I believe as you read these chapters you'll come to the conclusion they depict not some secret, magical methodology, but instead common sense. I urge you to read them more than once so they become not MY system but YOURS. There are three chapters in particular that are vital to becoming a persuasive leader through your speaking skills-Chapters 6, 9, and 10.

Chapter 6 shows how to draft backwards-what I refer to as the 3-1-2 Method, which is highly counter-intuitive. Since we were in elementary school, we have been taught to draft in a 1-2-3 manner-Introduction, Body, Conclusion. I have found that "backward drafting"-Conclusion (3), Introduction (1), Body (2) facilitates focus, thematic unity and keeps you within the time you have been given. It is the cornerstone of the S3PS System.

Chapters 9 and 10 outline a practice system I bring from the military-the Murder Board, a term which probably causes you to think of the old TV drama, *The Sopranos*. I liken it to aviation's Flight Simulator. In that simulated cockpit, pilots learn on the ground how to deal with emergencies at 35,000 feet. The Murder Board helps presenters hone speaking skills and anticipate questions and objections.

A side benefit of this practice method is that it reduces "fear of speaking" by building your confidence that you will not be caught flat-footed with a question. An effective Murder Board will result in the unknown becoming the known.

I have placed two articles *Taming Hostile Audiences: Persuading Those Who Would Rather Jeer Than Cheer* and *Model for Winning Oral Presentations: The Philly Cheesesteak* as Appendices to demonstrate how the S3P3 System can be applied to distinct types of presentations. I did not want to include them as chapters so as to not disrupt the flow of the Three Ps. Both articles were widely published, and they will reinforce the knowledge provided in the 21 chapters.

So, Game on! Start the journey to becoming an influential leader by improving your ability to persuade. Tony Robbins, the famed motivational speaker, has said persuasion is the most important skill a person can possess. He's spot on.

PART ONE

The S3P3 System

CHAPTER 1

Substance, Structure and Style

BECAUSE I HAVE put such emphasis on the S3P3 System you may think that this chapter of the Three S's and the following chapter on the Three Ps would be quite voluminous. Not so. These chapters will be rather sparse. The Three S's of this chapter should be thought of as the all-important pillars supporting the Three Ps which form a pyramid. Just a cursory outline is necessary here, especially as the remainder of this book will cover the Three P's.

But first ask yourself this question: "Are Speaking Skills Still Important in the Digital Age?"

As a speech coach my answer to that question is "They certainly are." Because you have acquired this book, you probably think so as well. But I wanted to see if there were valid arguments that technology had made the ability to present and persuade less important.

So, using this very technology, I asked the question on Google. To my surprise I found not one article claiming that speaking skills were less important in the 21st century. In fact I found several articles which posited that the very complexity of life today made the skill of clear, persuasive speaking even more important.

Let's take a look at what some key executives have said about presentation skills.

As I noted in the Prefaces, none other Jack Welch, former CEO of General Electric, wrote in *Published* in 2016

"…I've come to believe a person's skill in public speaking – be it in front of a crowd of 1,000 strangers or a meeting with five close associates – is more essential than ever. Making your case in writing is increasingly a thing of the past. You are what you say."

Welch's claim, that "making your case in writing" is increasingly a thing of the past" caught me by surprise. But then how often do you hear praise for a well-crafted memo compared to people marveling at a brilliant presentation? I'm not in complete agreement with Welch on the declining importance of writing skills, but his view certainly emphasizes how modern business does indeed value people who can "make their case" with their presentation skills.

Lee Iaccoca, former CEO of both Ford and Chrysler, in his 1984 autobiography said much the same thing as Welch:

" I've known a lot of engineers with brilliant minds who had trouble explaining them to others. It's always a shame to find people with great talent who can't explain to a board or committee what's in their heads."

A 2016 study by Burning Glass Technologies stated:

" Communication …[is] ranked as the most or second-most desired baseline skill in all industries. Organizational skills and writing abilities were also in high demand across the board and came in second and third among the most commonly requested skills by employers overall. Specifically, in Information Technology jobs communication skills and writing were the most sought after soft skills."

To see how timeless are the views of Welch, Iaccoca, and this Burning Glass study take a look at what one of the great leaders and orators of Ancient Greece, Pericles, said 2,500 years ago:

"Those who can think, but cannot express what they think, place on the level of those who cannot think."

When I came upon this quotation many years ago, I was so struck by it that I have it on my business card. I also use it frequently in my keynote presentations and workshops. It sums up the fact that great knowledge in your specialty is not sufficient. You must be able to communicate this knowledge clearly and persuasively to others.

How many times have you seen a person you knew to be an expert on an issue stumble through a presentation, failing to convey what he or she wanted the audience to understand?

Conversely, how many times have you seen a less capable person with a gift of gab mesmerize an audience? The goal must be to get the bright person's presentation skills near the level of his/her technical knowledge, to render YOUR presentation skills commensurate with your knowledge. That is my purpose in this book.

A company that certainly believes in the power of the presentation is McKinsey & Co., arguably the world's most renowned management consulting firm. The book, The McKinsey Mind, outlines the presentation methodology employed by this company, pointing out that its system is oriented toward the final presentation to the client. The book quotes numerous McKinsey "alumni," saying how they took the presenting system to their new firms and it gave them "unfair advantage."

One of these "graduates," Robert Garda, now a professor at Duke University's Fuqua School of Business, had this to say about the importance of presentation skills:

"I've put half-baked ideas into great presentations and seen them soar, and I've put great ideas into poor presentations, and watched them die."

There are many surveys where men and women in Information Technology (IT) testify that presentation skills are indeed vital for success. Ironically, these same surveys indicate many people will do all they can to avoid delivering a presentation. I'll discuss this "fear of speaking" in Chapter 11, showing how to channel this fear, making it into your ally.

Many speech coaches claim you cannot be a competent presenter until you "conquer the fear of speaking." I am not one of them. I believe this fear can be converted into enthusiasm and passion, prerequisites for not being a boring presenter.

I believe we can stipulate from the foregoing that the ability to be an excellent speaker is as important for success as it has always been. In the following pages you'll learn the S3P3 System comprised of *Substance, Structure* and *Style, Planning, Practicing* and *Presenting* that I developed and used in my speaking and speech coaching careers. It will provide a blueprint for successful and persuasive presentations.

Experienced writers and editors say every book has a "center:" the hub around which the rest of the book revolves. If that is so, this and the next chapter constitute the center of this book.

The S3P3 System is the method I used in delivering over 3,000 presentations--hundreds of them to very demanding, critical--and often hostile--audiences. It is the reason for any success I have had in speaking, and it is the method that I pass on in this book.

As social beings we spend the majority of our time communicating orally with other social beings. Writing is a more efficient way of expressing our ideas, but speaking is more effective and has greater impact on our reputations. Being able to express yourself is the best way to stand out from the crowd as the famed management expert, Peter Drucker, wrote many years ago:

"…the ability to express oneself is perhaps the most important of all the skills a person can possess."

While the thrust of this book is communicating effectively and persuasively to groups, the advice in these pages has equal applicability to one-on-one communications. The principles remain the same whether one is speaking to one person or a thousand people, as Jack Welch stated above.

Effective, persuasive communication is transferring information from your brain to the brains(s) of your audience in such a manner that this audience-- one or many--accepts your information as its own and buys in to what you are advocating. In effect, they persuade themselves because you have shown how their self-interest is served by adopting the position you have laid out.

To be able to do this your presentation requires focus, thematic unity and an in-depth knowledge of the concerns and problems of your audience so you can direct your message to hit these hot buttons. It also requires the ability to anticipate objections and questions the audience may have and the discipline to practice realistically.

To be a persuasive speaker who can "bring home the bacon" you must certainly "know your stuff." That is almost a truism although there are many people with more audacity than judgment who stand before a group with far less knowledge than prudence would dictate.

The majority of people who are called on to present are substantive experts and therein lies an essential problem. Some believe that technical knowledge is sufficient and they need not devote any attention to delivery skills for they consider themselves neither actors nor "talking dogs." I hope to persuade any of you who think that way that you must blend your knowledge with delivery skills.

So let's take a look at these six elements which constitute the S3P3 System. The three S's may be thought of as pillars which support the pyramid of the three P's.

SUBSTANCE

Mastery of the subject is an absolute necessity for any speaker. You must have a clearly defined objective and focused research. This does not mean only compilation of factual data. You need an active and comprehensive knowledge of the subject at issue in order to respond to challenges from the audience, especially if the audience might be predisposed to disagree.

Only a solid grasp of the subject matter can save a presenter when confronted with an unexpected question or objection from the audience. However, substance without structure or style can make the presentation an incoherent, boring recitation of data.

STRUCTURE

The human mind possesses a certain data-processing logic. The speaker who is aware of how people process information and how new data is either accepted or rejected can learn to structure a presentation so as to facilitate comprehension.

The knowledge of the audience's self-interest--"What's in it for me?"--is an essential tool for structuring a presentation, so it hits the target of the collective mind of audience members, leading these people to persuade themselves and buy in to what you are advocating.

STYLE

This is the most frequently ignored part of the speaking art by substantive experts, possibly because it has the connotation of show business. It refers to word choice, body language, movement and vocal quality.

Style is that almost indefinable quality of a speaker that causes audience members, even those opposed to the issue being "sold," to listen, not be bored and to open their minds. Another word of caution: style without substance can expose the speaker to the charge of being shallow.

In the next chapter we'll look briefly at the three levels of the pyramid of Planning, Practicing and Presenting. I say briefly, because the remaining nineteen chapters will cover the Three P's in depth.

CHAPTER 2

Planning, Practicing and Presenting

THINK OF THE Three P's described here as a pyramid, from the base of Planning to the vital middle stage of Practicing to the apex of Presenting. The three steps are both systematic and systemic, for how you plan determines how you will practice, which naturally influences how you will present.

PLANNING

Planning is the wide base required of any stable structure and any good presentation. It is the single most important building element of any presentation. Unfortunately, most presentations are done with an inverted pyramid as the model, with the narrow base indicating little planning and practice, thus placing all the weight on the presentation. This lack of planning frequently results in poor presentations.

Good business sense dictates that the same effort which goes into the development of a product, policy, or service be devoted to the presentation whose purpose is selling this product, policy, or service. The planning stage is where the presenter develops a strategy, a game plan, a frame of reference and a point of view for the presentation.

An important part of the planning process is gathering "Audience Intelligence:" information about the concerns, problems, attitudes and expectations of the group of people whom you are about to face in your presentation. Because the speaker must mesh his or her objective for the presentation with the audience's needs and concerns, the more time spent on strategic planning, the easier will be the actual presentation. Thorough planning lays the groundwork for a successful presentation.

PRACTICING

After you have completed the planning stage you are now ready to start practicing. This is an orderly means to internalize the presentation. You will take some of the apprehension out of the experience by anticipating reactions, comments and questions and by developing appropriate responses.

The key to smart practicing is a "Murder Board," a realistic simulation of the presentation which I bring from the military. You conduct it in front of a suitable audience--e.g., colleagues, relatives, friends-- who can put your knowledge to the test. I'll cover this method in detail in Chapters 9 and 10.

Your confidence zooms when you have gone through a practice phase that enables you to say, "I know this subject better than anyone in the audience. I want them to take their best shot because I'll be able to answer any question thrown at me!" That is the attitude you want to carry with you into the presentation.

PRESENTING

Finally, you reach that apex: the actual presentation. This is the payoff for the time you have spent assuring that you have included all the required substance, placed it within a structure that facilitates audience comprehension and agreement with the position you are advocating and that you have done it with the style most appropriate to make your presentation memorable and successful.

If you have (1) done the planning, to include Audience Intelligence collection, and developed a focus that meshes with audience members' needs and concerns and (2) practiced with focus to include an intensive simulation enabling you to anticipate questions and objections, you are ready for "show time."

PART TWO

Planning

CHAPTER 3

Acquiring Macro and Micro Intelligence on Audience Members

V IRTUALLY ALL SPEECH coaches emphasize that the presentation must not be about the speaker but about the audience. As a speaker you must learn the audience's concerns, wants, problems. But how do you learn these concerns, wants, problems? By a systematic method of collecting intelligence on the members of the audience. I submit this must be done on two levels which I'll explain below.

First, let me get a couple of nomenclature biases of mine out of the way. I don't like the oft-used term "audience analysis." It reminds me of high school students dissecting a frog. Audience members are human beings, each with his or her own feelings, beliefs, prejudices. Additionally, I dislike using the word "audience." It is a collective, but the unwary may think of that group as a single entity. The reality, of course, is that an audience is composed of individuals. A presentation to 100 people is therefore a presentation to 100 audiences, as each person will perceive the presentation differently. I prefer the term "Audience Intelligence collection," which I divide into Macro and Micro Intelligence.

Macro Intelligence is the information which is easily obtained: the audience size and the demographics--ages, educational levels, how many men, how many women, etc. It is useful and as a speaker you must, as a minimum, have this information. You can acquire it by telephone conversations with the organizers, Internet research, Google searches, reading company reports and the like.

Micro Intelligence, while more difficult to obtain than the macro variety, is much more useful. It drills down to attitudes of audience members, what issues are important to them, what are their needs and problems, are there people who are likely to interrupt and be disruptive. In short, the more intelligence of this type, the more likely it is you can intersect your objective with the needs of audience members. You are collecting needed information on audience members so you can focus your presentation on solving their problems.

What are their views/ objections to the issue you are addressing? You need this information so you can mesh your objectives as speaker with the psychological and informational needs of your audience members. Your objective must be to "write on the brains" of audience members with your ideas so they do indeed buy in to your position. This requires that you know the problems confronting these people.

This Micro Intelligence is much easier to acquire in the age of social media than it was in earlier years. Twitter, Facebook, Instagram, and other social networks can be a mother lode of information.

The fundamental reason people listen to a presentation is to gain information that will solve a problem, fill an informational need and give them an "edge." As a presenter, you must realize this at the outset. Attempting to impress audience members with your erudition or with the features of your product or service will fall on deaf ears if you do not show how this product or service will help these audience members.

How I avoided an Ambush with Micro Intelligence

Let me use a personal example showing the value of Micro Intelligence. Just after I was assigned to the State Department to debate US policy in Central America around the country, I was asked by Public Affairs to speak at a West Coast university to a group of approximately 300 students and residents of the nearby town. I agreed and called the student who had made the request. Good thing I did.

After a pleasant chat he revealed, perhaps inadvertently, that I would not be the only speaker but instead be part of a panel with three academic experts on Latin America. He also told me the sponsoring group was called "Students for a Sane Policy in Central America"--a pretty good clue that they did not think much of US policy.

Sensing this event would not be a walk in the park, I told him I'd come out a day earlier than planned and suggested we have pizza and beer to discuss the event and for him to bring a couple of friends. I'd pick up the tab.

I had access to the State Department LexisNexis account in those pre-Google days and reviewed recent articles written by the three professors who would be my co-panelists. As I expected, they were all critical of US policy in the region and I assumed (correctly as it turned out) these articles reflected the positions they would take as their game plan in the panel discussion. This was invaluable Micro Intelligence. They, of course, would know my game plan: US policy.

When the three students and I met for our pizza and beer we had good-natured jousting on US policy. I was able to clarify some of their misperceptions and they came to see me as human being, not a remote corporate figure from Washington. I also picked up valuable information on the audience.

The night of the event went as I believed it would, thanks to gaining that Micro Intelligence. The professors seemed flattered--and somewhat surprised--that I had read their articles, even as I pointed out what I demonstrated were serious inaccuracies. I acknowledged problems in our policy and elucidated the efforts we were making to correct the human rights abuses being committed by the countries we were supporting.

I emphasized that the Sandinistas in Nicaragua were in fact a military dictatorship, with an Army far greater in size than the neighboring countries and were being supplied by the Soviet Union, not exactly a paragon of democracy. This caused the professors some anguish because their careers as Latin American specialists had been spent as critics of military dictatorships. Now they were in the position of defending one, requiring some interesting verbal gymnastics. I even had some of the audience laughing at the inconsistency of the professors. I believe I gained some support for our policy. However, if I had not gained that Micro Intelligence flowing from my phone call, the night would have been a total disaster.

Now, let's return to the key parts of Micro Intelligence and look at what elements you require in the planning phase.

HOW MUCH DO AUDIENCE MEMBERS KNOW ABOUT THE ISSUE?

It is imperative that you not waste an audience's time with details already known to these people. You want your presentation to add to the net knowledge they possess. At the same time, you do not want to assume audience members know as much about the subject as you do.

Threading your way between these two extremes, while difficult, is required for those wishing to deliver a successful presentation. The best way is to aim slightly above the level of knowledge you believe the audience has on the subject. Better to have them reach than for them to think you are talking down to them.

DO AUDIENCE MEMBERS EXPECT AN OVERVIEW OR DETAILED PRESENTATION?

Another important element of this stage is determining audience expectations. Are they expecting an overview of the issue, with follow-up detail to be provided in written material, or is this a "roll up the sleeves, give us all the information you have" group?"

ARE AUDIENCE MEMBERS OPEN-MINDED OR OPINIONATED?

Few people are completely open-minded, as they have points of view on the issue. Their self-interest, however, will cause them to shift positions if your presentation shows the benefits that will accrue to them if they adopt your view.

Those who are strongly opposed to what you are "selling" will be a tougher nut to crack. Look for some common ground and perhaps you can lessen this opposition, as well as pointing out, in a subtle manner, how their position might be in contrast to their value system.

Who makes the decisions, and who influences him or her?

In most business or government presentations the decision-maker will be the ranking person. It is this person who should, of course, be the target of your presentation. You should also learn before the presentation whom this person leans on for advice. A phone call or meeting with this person could facilitate having that advice support your position.

Are there any "troublemakers" in the audience?

There are some people who delight in showing off their knowledge by harassing the presenter. Find out who these people are before the presentation, stroke their delicate egos by asking for their input ahead of time, then mention them during your presentation. They will be less likely to cause trouble.

In Chapter 4 I will emphasize that a presentation is a social contract between speaker and audience members. Speakers must realize that they have an obligation to these audience members to be honest, not deceptive, and to provide the information that can best solve the problem (s) of audience members.

CHAPTER 4

Your Obligations as a Presenter

Audience members should pay attention and listen to the argument the presenter is making, but they certainly do not always do so. Presenters, however, must make every effort to be professional and courteous. Here are six elements I believe you, as a presenter/speaker, are obliged to fulfill.

1. Solve the Audience's Problems

The fundamental reason people listen to presentations is to gain information that will solve a problem, fill an informational need and give them an "edge." Attempting to impress your audience with your erudition or with the features of your product or service will not be heard if you don't show how this information will help audience members.

Acquiring maximum information on audience members is absolutely essential for an effective and persuasive presentation. As pointed out in Chapter 3, seek especially to learn the problems faced by the audience so you can construct a presentation that shows how these problems can be solved.

2. Get to the point early

Because of the overwhelming demands on our time and the multi–tasking we are all involved in, none of us has the patience to listen to a presentation that appears to be a mystery novel. Your audience members want an idea of the route you are taking and the eventual destination. Drafting backwards in the 3-1-2 method, which will be illustrated in Chapter 6, will help you achieve focus and indeed "Get to the point." If the audience is mystified as to where you are taking them in this journey, they will probably tune out early. If you are going to solve problems, let your listeners know up front that you know what these problems are and let them know you have a solution.

3. Give audience members "presentation ammunition"

Everyone must present to someone higher in the corporate food chain. In a sales context, if you are presenting to a person who does not have the power to authorize a purchase, keep that person's boss in mind as you are preparing your presentation. Without being too obvious, provide the person who lacks the buying/decision power with ammunition he or she can use when making your case further up the pecking order. You'll be gaining points with this person, as you will be making him or her look smart in front of the boss.

4. Provide maximum relevant data

For the same reason that you wish to get to the point early, you must also avoid doing a "data dump" on your listeners. They only want information which will solve their problem.

The more words and facts you present the greater the likelihood that your essential message will be lost. Short-term memory is precisely that. As new information is presented it tends to push the just heard information out, somewhat akin to the First In, First Out (FIFO) accounting method.

If, however, the factual information is tied to the needs, wants and concerns of the audience--its problems--then audience members will retain the information most relevant to their needs and problems.

Presenting this relevant data in such a way that it will be retained is a function of structure. I'll discuss how to develop a tested and proven method to develop this all–important structure of the presentation in Chapter 6.

A word of caution, however. Despite the importance of structuring your information in a logical, coherent manner, structure alone is not enough. A presentation can have superb structure and still fail if it is delivered by a boring presenter.

If, on the other hand, you go over the allotted time, you will be considered inefficient and you will have stolen audience members' most valuable commodity: their time.

Here's a tip. Have a colleague sit behind the audience, or in the rear of the room, and give you unobtrusive signals when you hit "three minutes left" and "one minute left." Avoid looking at your watch. Although glancing at your watch demonstrates you are sensitive to the time needs of the audience, it can also cause members of the audience to shift their attention from the substance of your presentation to the question, "How much longer will this go on?"

In certain scored situations, such as a proposal for venture capital, or an oral presentation for a government contract, presenters are penalized for going beyond the time limit and could easily lose the capital infusion or contract they are seeking, no matter how superior their product, service or innovative idea.

5. PRESENT IN CLEAREST TERMS POSSIBLE

When we wish to provide the maximum relevant data in minimum time there is the temptation to speak rapidly. Nerves can also cause rapid speaking. This becomes especially critical when the information being presented is complex and the audience needs time to absorb it. You must also take into account the knowledge level of the issue and if there are audience members for whom English is a second language. In Chapter 12, I'll discuss the need for clarity in more detail. In the following Chapter 5, we'll cover the techniques of drafting your presentation.

CHAPTER 5

Tricks of the Drafting Trade

BECAUSE WORDS ARE the vehicles by which we transmit our thoughts to others and because we receive more formal training in writing than speaking there is an understandable tendency to draft a presentation as if we were writing a memo or essay. The emphasis from grade school to college is on the written, not the spoken, word. Speaking is considered a natural process but writing well is a discipline replete with rules and conventions.

Far more emphasis is placed in our years of formal education on strengthening our written communication skills. We certainly cannot write as automatically as we can speak. We start to communicate and persuade orally as soon as we leave our mother's womb but we only start to learn how to express our thoughts in writing in the first grade. As a result of so much training in writing and so little in speaking we frequently fall back on the lessons learned about writing when we are called on to make a spoken presentation. That is a mistake.

HOW WRITING AND SPEAKING DIFFER

Because of this emphasis in writing over speaking, we must always be alert that the two disciplines are significantly different. In effect, to be a good speaker you have to "unlearn" many of the rules and conventions about writing so that you do not deliver an oral essay which might look good to the eye on paper but might not sound good to the ear when heard by your audience. It is how audience members hear you that determines how they will accept your message. Whenever preparing an oral presentation, your target is the ear, not the eye.

When Ted Sorenson, President John F. Kennedy's speech writer, finished the first draft of a speech the President was to deliver, he would come to the Oval Office and read it to JFK. The President wanted to hear how the phrases sounded, just as his audiences would hear his speech. Follow Kennedy's lesson and, after you have drafted your presentation, read it into an audio recorder, then listen. Do you sound natural and conversational or stilted and excessively formal? If you cringe at how you sound, work on your inflection, on your pacing, on eliminating, or at least reducing, the "uh's" and "y'knows" that plague so many speakers. The remainder of this chapter contains tips to help you make your presentation play better to the ear, even if on paper it does not look as good to the eye as a well-crafted essay.

OPTIONS FOR DRAFTING THE PRESENTATION

The most tedious part of preparing a presentation is certainly the drafting stage. It brings to mind the writer's lament, "I love having written, but I hate writing." There are three approaches to take in drafting a presentation, and they can be combined.

VERBATIM

Writing your presentation out as an essay has the advantage of assuring that most of the key points will be covered. The fundamental disadvantage to this practice is that you will use words and syntax more appropriate for the written medium and not the more conversational style of the oral presentation. Other disadvantages of the verbatim draft are: (1) If taken to the lectern, it becomes a crutch. This may cause the speaker to (2) read the presentation which in turn will result in (3) falling back on our habit to speak in a mind-numbing monotone and at the much faster silent reading speed.

OUTLINE

Although the outline is the form we are normally most comfortable with, logical fallacies can creep into the presentation and key points could be omitted. But it is time-saving and has the advantage of drafting closer to the manner in which we speak and which the audience listens to most easily.

MEMORY JOGGERS

Placing key points on 3x5 cards is an excellent time-saving device when you are in full command of the data. The disadvantage is that you may omit key points "in the heat of battle" or even when you are in the drafting stage.

It's best to combine all three of these methods if you have the time. Write out the initial draft verbatim, then reduce it to an outline and, finally, place the key points of the outline on 3x5 cards.

Because of repetition, going through this procedure has the added benefit of allowing you to internalize the data more readily. You will also find that you will make only minimum use even of your "memory joggers" when you are actually delivering the presentation. Moreover, you'll find that your self-confidence in speaking to a group increases dramatically as you become more assured of your command of the data.

TECHNIQUES OF DRAFTING

Use contractions. When we write, we have been schooled to put on paper phrases such as "We do not..." If we use this rule when making a presentation, the tendency will be to sound somewhat stuffy. It is better in a presentation to say "We don't.." because that's how we would probably express the thought in a conversation. Speaking today is actually a conversation, not a dissertation.

Presidents of the United States, and their speech writers, avoid the written style when making a speech, no matter how weighty the issue. These leaders recognize the need for a conversational tone to connect with the American people. Use short, even one-sentence, paragraphs.

When you took writing courses in high school and college, a red pencil was probably applied generously by the teacher or professor to a paper with one-sentence paragraphs. Doubtless you were taught that a paragraph is comprised of 4 or 5 sentences. But in a spoken presentation, a one-sentence paragraph adds punch to your thoughts.

Be repetitive. In writing, economy of words is a principle and excessive repetition would draw the ire and red pencil of that same teacher. In speaking, however, repetition of key thoughts and ideas is necessary because audiences tune in and tune out. In a written document, a reader, when distracted or sleepy, can put down the paper and then pick it up later. In the oral presentation there is no instant replay, so the speaker, aware of the likelihood that listeners will drift off, must repeat the key points, using slightly different phrases to express the same point.

THE CELLULAR PHONE

When the muse strikes, use your cellular phone. Once you start the drafting process you'll find the creative juices flow at unexpected moments. Let's say you are driving in congested traffic when a brilliant idea for your presentation comes to you. How can you capture this inspiration from the right brain?

You can't write it down if you are driving, and you probably don't have an audio recorder handy. Pull over to the side of the road and leave a voice mail or your land line. Your spontaneous brilliance has been captured for posterity, there for you to include in your presentation. I can't count the number of times I have done this, even walking down the street. No one thinks you are weird because nowadays everybody is used to people talking on their phones.

USE SIMPLE LANGUAGE

The people in your audience will not have access to a dictionary, consequently try to not impress these people with your vocabulary. When an audience member is trying to remember what a particular word means he or she will be missing what you are saying next. Sir

Winston Churchill was an advocate of the simple word and the short sentence. His speeches are masterpieces of communication.

In Chapter 6, we'll show you how to eliminate drafting by the traditional 1-2-3 method (Introduction-Body-Conclusion) which you have probably used all your life, and replace it with the much more functional 3-1-2 method (Conclusion-Introduction-Body) which is the heart of the S3P3 System. Counter-intuitive though it may, be, this "Backward Drafting" is far more effective in organizing the thoughts you want to convey to your audience.

CHAPTER 6

Drafting Backwards: The 3-1-2 System

A WARNING. THIS IS perhaps the most densely-packed chapter. Now that you have learned the mechanics of drafting your presentation it is time to turn the process on its head. I learned the concept of "Backward Planning" in training at Fort Benning, Georgia. You plan not from the beginning, but backwards from the objective you wish to accomplish. This concept had a profound impact on my speaking and eventually became the underpinning for my career as a speech coach. I found that this reverse approach increased both focus and thematic unity in my workshops for my "students."

All you need is counter-intuitive thinking, a stack of 3x5 cards, and the 3-1-2 System.

What are the benefits of this system? Backward Planning makes it less likely that you will go off on an audience-confusing tangent. You will be able to structure your presentation so the audience members know where you are taking them. The 3-1-2 System is analogous to the flight plan a pilot files before taking off. You begin with the end in mind.

THE 3-1-2 SYSTEM AND THE PRIMACY AND RECENCY EFFECT

The S3P3 System is rooted in the Primacy and Recency Effect. Postulated by New Zealand psychologist, Dr. Frederick Hansen Lund, in 1925, the Law of Primacy, also known as the Primacy Effect, holds that the side of an argument presented first will have greater effectiveness in persuasion--i.e., will be better remembered or believed--than the side subsequently presented. Synonymously referred to as the Primacy-Recency Effect, it can be broken down into two elements. The Recency Effect means that upon hearing a long list of words you will be more likely to remember the words you heard at the end of the list than those occurring in the middle while the Primacy Effect means that you will be more likely to remember words you heard at the beginning of the list than those in the middle.

The Primacy-Recency Effect, often called the Law of Primacy and the Law of Recency, has many applications, including but not limited to the court room. It is heavily utilized in cross-examination, jury selection and many other elements of trial law, where it certainly is the game plan for trial attorneys.

Let me illustrate with an example from one of the most famous court room dramas in recent history: "The Trial of the 20th Century" in 1995--that of O.J. Simpson. Shortly after the conclusion of that trial and its controversial verdict, a noted trial attorney was on a television program strongly criticizing the prosecution team of the Los Angeles District Attorney's office. He said he had learned that Marcia Clark, the lead prosecutor, had started preparing her closing argument the night before she delivered it. The non-lawyer host asked, "Well, when she should she have started preparing it?" The lawyer exploded, "Before the trial began!" He went on to say that he knew for a fact that Simpson's defense attorney, Johnnie Cochran, had started preparing his closing argument as soon as he became a member of the defense team. As I listened to the famous lawyer's comments, I felt my 3-1-2 system to be validated.

My first exposure to the Primacy-Recency Law had come a few years earlier. I had written an essay, "The Art of Making Winning Presentations," which was my first full exposition of the 3-1-2 system.

I sent it to an old Army friend who was now heading a successful law firm. He called me the next day asking for permission to make copies to distribute to the lawyers in his firm, saying the essay contained excellent advice for those engaged in litigation.

He added that it was clear to him that I was a "Primacist." Knowing I didn't have the slightest idea what he meant, he explained the Primacy and Recency concept. He added that there were strong differences of opinion among legal scholars on whether Opening statements or Closing arguments were more important and law journals were replete with learned articles on the subject, arguing which was more important-the Opening Statement or the Closing Argument.

Primacy and Recency are just as important for a presenter as they are for a trial lawyer. Audiences and juries alike can remember what they hear first and last but might not recall much of what they hear in between. If you do not grab the audience's attention with a strong opening, a dynamite closing will have less impact because the audience might not have been inspired to listen to the factual data leading up to the conclusion. So, too, with juries.

The overriding advantage of applying the Primacy and Recency/3-1-2 Concept to delivering presentations is that it helps develop both focus and thematic unity. If you first develop your conclusion--the equivalent of the lawyer's closing argument--by means of the 3-1-2 method, then you know how the presentation will end.

A presenter must always accommodate the information to be presented to the time to be allocated for the presentation. By initially developing your "Bottom Line Conclusion," you can build backwards in a time-efficient manner. Doing so also provides you with a mini-presentation if the time allocated is suddenly reduced. I'll address that contingency in the next chapter about the need to be prepared with a Plan B. Presentations today must get to the point, focus on the needs of the audience and be easily-understood by audience members. These tasks are the responsibility of the presenter.

Time is the defining aspect of any presentation. Few audiences have the time for a full exposition of a subject. The presenter must distill the salient data into an easily and quickly understood message.

The 3-1-2 System will enable you to organize your thoughts in the optimum manner in order to implant your message in the collective mind of the audience.

Let's say you have been tasked to make an important presentation to your boss, or a board of directors, or perhaps an important client. You are told you will have twenty minutes to make your case. You prepare in the traditional way, which I'll call the 1-2-3 System of Introduction, Body, and Conclusion. You practice diligently, develop excellent visuals and have edited your presentation to just under twenty minutes. Comes the big day and you show up at the appropriate location on time, only to be told that, because of extenuating circumstances--schedule conflicts, unforeseen delays, etc.--you will have only five minutes to make your presentation. Now the pressure is on you to make a dramatic adjustment. You have a few options.

First, you can say, "Sorry, my presentation simply cannot be done in five minutes. Call me when they have the time to listen to the entire presentation." This may not be a career-enhancing option. Second, you can try to speak rapidly, enabling you to get maximum information into that minimum time allotted you, but these senior executives will probably think you are a blabbering idiot. Third, as you are approaching the audience--be it one person or a group--you desperately try to think of the most important part of your presentation. It's not likely you will be able to do so because you have prepared from the front, not the back.

You are not alone. Most people prepare their presentations using a 1-2-3 method described previously. They draft in the order of how they will deliver: (1) Introduction (2) Body and (3) Conclusion. This is the method to organize our thoughts which we have been taught since elementary school. Unfortunately, this system leads to various false starts because the presenter is attempting to place the ten gallons of knowledge he or she possesses on the subject into the eight-ounce glass of the presentation. It is definitely not flexible and forces the presenter to make changes on the fly. This may result in time-pressed presentations lacking coherence. In effect, the traditional system of organizing our thoughts is simply not geared to presentations in the 21st century.

THE 3-1-2 ALTERNATIVE

Let's wake up from that nightmare scenario described above, which, of course, is the way things generally work. If you had instead prepared your presentation with the seven-step 3-1-2 System outlined below, you would have been unflustered when asked to reduce your twenty minute presentation to five minutes-you would have already done so in your planning and practicing stages.

The 3-1-2 System will enable you to condense voluminous content you possess as an expert into the limited amount of time your audience has to listen to you. You'll have more focus because you will know where you are going in the presentation. Most importantly, your audience will see a structure to your presentation that will enable them to follow and, in the best of cases, ultimately agree with your argument. The 3-1-2 System is counter-intuitive but it most certainly results in a more focused presentation which can easily be adjusted. Here are seven steps you can follow to get off on the right foot in preparing any presentation.

1. Place a 30-60 second "Bottom Line" of your message on a 3x5 card. You have gained intelligence on audience needs and problems; you have a specific objective. The words which you believe will result in the intersection of the audience's needs and your objective goes on this card which you mark with a 3.

2. Place in front of this phrase words that signal the close of your presentation, such as: "So, in conclusion" or "Let me leave you with this thought." You now have the words which will get you off the stage. This is your closing argument, to use the lawyer's term. It can also provide you with a mini-presentation when you face that dramatic reduction of time for your presentation noted above.

3. Take another 3x5 card, mark it with a 1 and write an opening phrase that will motivate the audience to listen to you because you have hit a psychological "hot button" that sends the signal to the audience, "This will benefit me" or "This will keep me out of trouble." A startling statistic or an apt quotation from a

well-known (to the audience) figure could also be in this beginning as an attention-getter.

4. An alternative and effective technique is to summarize your 3 card conclusion in your opening statement, and then inform the audience that you will now proceed to prove the validity of your conclusion.

5. Audience members now know where you are going and can, in effect, open the "files" on their mental desktops to absorb this information. Remember that a business presentation is not a mystery novel. You want your audience to know "Who shot John?" right away and then you want to show the evidence. Above all, you want your audience members to be alerted to the fact that you know their material or psychological needs/problems and are prepared to provide information which addresses these concerns.

6. With the 3 and 1 cards filled out you have the parameters of your presentation established and this will help you in the drafting stage as you develop the body of your presentation in 2. Most importantly, you will avoid going off on a tangent or confusing your audience with too much detail.

7. You know where you are going, and can thus structure your presentation so the audience can know where you are taking them. Take a few cards, marked 2A, 2B, 2C, etc. and list your supporting arguments.

The 3-1-2 System ensures that the most important information you wish the audience to retain and act upon is placed at the beginning and at the end. The 3-1-2 System is a great improvement on the traditional 1-2-3 system of drafting that you have probably used most of your life.

At the risk of redundancy, here is a summary of alternate ways for opening and closing your presentation.

OPENING

1. Begin with a question that relates to the principal problem/concern of the audience.

2. Begin with a relevant quotation from a prominent person known to audience members.

3. Begin with your conclusion/solution, telling audience members you'll now show how you arrived at that conclusion.

CLOSING

1. Send the signal you are about to close with a phrase such as "In conclusion…".

2. Ask for action such as project approval, support for policy, etc.

3. Refer back to how you opened, showing how you have now provided information that helps solve the problem.

4. Increase the volume of your voice, use emphatic body language to supplement your factual knowledge.

One of the principal benefits of organizing with the 3-1-2 System is sparing you from the situation described above where a last-minute schedule change drastically reduces the amount of time you have available for your presentation. The 3-1-2 System will ensure you are well prepared to make the most of your allocated time when you must go to Plan B, which I'll cover in Chapter: 7.

CHAPTER 7

Just in Case! The Plan B Draft

I N A PERFECT world, presenters would have the time to deliver their presentation in its entirety. In the real world of the 21st century, however, it is more the rule than the exception that time will be dramatically reduced from that originally allocated for a presentation.

PRESENTATIONS AND TIME

A challenge that confronts all presenters, therefore, is time. Audience members may originally have time for a full-blown presentation, then those minutes could be reduced at the last minute. Yet the presenter still has the obligation to provide the information required by the audience.

Question: How can such last-minute schedule changes to presentations be accommodated?

Answer: Have a Plan B, a reduced version of your presentation, ready when you walk into the room. You do not want to be in the position of frantically revising your notes and visuals while your audience watches. The old Boy Scout motto, "Be Prepared," will serve you well.

Generally, the later in the day a presentation is scheduled, the higher the probability is that the time for the presentation will be severely reduced. You may get apologies for putting you in such a position. Nevertheless, it is your responsibility to provide maximum information, in minimum time and in the clearest manner possible, no matter the circumstances under which you must make the presentation. This means that you must plan for the very real possibility that you will have less time than you thought you would. Thus the need for the Plan B presentation.

HOW TO DEVELOP THE PLAN B PRESENTATION

To clarify terms, let's consider your Plan A presentation as the one you are planning to deliver within the time limits you have been told you will have. The Plan B presentation is the one you may have to deliver within last minute time constraints.

Constructing your presentation with the 3–1–2 System facilitates adjusting to last minute changes in the schedule that result in having your allotted time reduced. The components of the 3–1–2 planning and drafting process—3) Conclusion– 1) Opening-2)Body--allow you to build the Plan A and the Plan B presentations simultaneously. The result is a presentation that can be easily expanded or, more likely, contracted.

THE NEED FOR CARDS

To ensure maximum flexibility, 3x5 cards are preferable, but, if desired, a larger size is acceptable. Be aware that using a large paper size, such as 8.5x11 sheets, in a presentation would make adding or deleting optional elements too cumbersome.

The cards should be marked to show their priority. I use a red felt tip pen to show "absolutely needed", green for "very useful" and blue for "nice to have."

Write in large letters, and put a sequential numbering system on the cards. Your objective must be to find the cards quickly so you can organize your "new" presentation rapidly. Additionally, having the cards numbered will help you get back on track if they fall to the floor.

THE 3 AND 1 FOUNDATION

The 3 card, as we discussed in the last chapter, is the Bottom Line: the words that will answer the fundamental question of all audience members, "What's in it for me?"

The 1 card contains the opening that motivates audience members to listen and to conclude immediately that their problem can be solved by this presentation. It is this Return On Investment (ROI) opening which provokes audience members to pay attention because of self–interest.

There should be such a logical connection between the 1 and 3 cards that, when time is reduced to one minute or less, these two statements can comprise the entire presentation. It is maximum information in minimum time and in the clearest form possible.

All presentations, consequently, require the 3 and 1 components, although in extreme cases there could be such a time constraint that only the Bottom Line Conclusion, or 3, is articulated.

THE PLAN B CONTINGENCY

Now we come to the Plan B contingency. When you are developing your main supporting points, the various 2 cards--viz., 2A, 2B, 2C, etc.--provide the logical scaffolding for the presentation.

For maximum flexibility, organize your presentation so that the various 2 cards have their own supporting evidence such as "nice to know" but not "need to know." For example, you will have a card marked 2A, a principal supporting pillar of your presentation, which is in turn supported by cards marked 2A i, 2A ii, 2A iii, etc. Do the same with the 2B and 2C cards. Dividing your supporting evidence into these sub-categories will enable you to reduce your presentation as time demands. You can delete the i, ii and iii cards if you do not have the time for the full presentation. Although reduced, the presentation maintains its internal consistency and coherence.

PLAN B AND POWERPOINT

Have separate disks and/or thumb sticks for your original, full-length presentation and for the Plan B presentation. Just substitute one for the other and you are in good shape. Alternatively, you can have a paper or card next to the projector listing the number of each of the Plan B slides. When presenting, just hit the number of the slide and the return button and PowerPoint will show only those slides which are pertinent to the Plan B presentation.

HOW PLAN B CAN HELP YOU

The obvious benefit of developing a contingency plan for a reduced presentation is to provide your audience members with information they require despite the reduced time.

There is an added benefit for the presenter who delivers an excellent presentation under such difficult circumstances. If you can appear to be unflustered by the changed situation and move effortlessly into the reduced time you will appear as a person who has his or her act together, a skill that will transcend the presentation itself. You will appear organized and professional. It will demonstrate to, say, superiors in your organization or company, that you can operate under pressure and have the ability to think ahead--a highly valued trait. So having your time reduced may not be such a bad thing to happen after all.

In Part, 3, we'll move from the written word to the spoken word in systematic practicing.

PART THREE

Practicing

CHAPTER 8

The Practice Two-Step

VIRTUALLY ALL SPEECH coaches advocate significant practice time for would-be presenters before they step in front of an audience. Most of the books and articles emphasize the need for practicing by one's self initially and subsequently with one or two colleagues.

I certainly agree with the need for intensive practice but I differ from many of my colleagues in that I believe the most beneficial practice comes in front of a simulated audience, not alone in front of a mirror or video camera, or even before one person. When I read these books and articles specifying how people preparing to present must listen to their vocal inflection, observe their body language, control their breathing, etc., all the while converting their written outline of verbatim text to the spoken language, I think that's overwhelming. And it just won't work.

We are, as Aristotle said, social animals, and getting human feedback in a realistic environment is the best way for presenters to prepare. Hence my three-step practice system, which I followed "in real life" and now pass on to my clients, places much more emphasis on the the third step--the "Murder Board"--than I do on the solo practice or the practice with one person. Both have value, but primarily as a way to the third step.

In this short chapter I'll set the stage for the all-important final stage of practicing your presentation with the rather macabre name, "Murder Board" which, as I said previously, I bring from the military. We'll cover it in detail in Chapter 9. First, however we'll discuss briefly those two steps which precede it--Step One: Practicing solo and Step Two: Practicing with one person..

STEP ONE: PRACTICING SOLO

Now that you have the draft of your presentation developed with the 3-1-2 system--either verbatim or with an outline/3x5 cards method--and have developed a Plan B if things don't go as planned, it is time to convert those written words to the spoken. Remember, you are not writing a memo. You are preparing to have your voice carry the message.

You should have no one near you for your initial solo practice. You will be at your weakest as you start to speak aloud the words in your draft, replete with "uh's" and "y'knows." Observing how another person is reacting, perhaps a colleague, may damage your confidence.

Many books on presentation skills/public speaking advise to practice in front of a mirror so you can observe your gestures and any distracting mannerisms. When I first started coaching I also advised clients to do this. Soon, however, I concluded it was terrible advice. The objective of this first step is to cement the words you have written in your brain. Watching yourself in a mirror will lessen your focus on those words.

Seeing and hearing yourself in this practice session, however, is vital so you can improve. Instead of a mirror, use a video camera or smart phone. When appropriate, smile. When delivering somber news make sure you have a somber look on your face. Audiences will note any inconsistency between content and non-verbal signals.

Listen for the rate of delivery. A comfortable rate is about 150 words per minute. A bit faster can connote enthusiasm, which is good, but a consistent "machine-gun" delivery will overwhelm an audience. Speaking too slowly could put your audience to sleep. Concentrate on removing the "uh's" and "y'knows" by substituting a pause. If you are speaking in a monotone, use a high lighter or pen to underline on your notes those words that demand inflection, such as "excited" or "generated."

Recording your solo practice by means of an audio recorder, video camera or smart phone will allow you to see and hear yourself as your audience will see and hear you. A warning: hearing your voice on a recording can be disconcerting. You'll say, "That's not how I sound!" But that is how you sound and how audience members will hear you.

Why is your "electronic" voice--and the one audience members hear-- different from the voice you hear every day? It is because when you hear yourself speaking you are listening on two channels: the words coming out of your mouth and the vibrations being transmitted to your inner ear and resonating via the boney structure of your cranium. That combination makes your voice appear more resonant, less nasal and lower pitch-sounding--to you. But audience members are not receiving the bone-caused vibrations. So what you hear on a recording is close to what your audience members are actually hearing when you speak. Just get used to it. You will.

What about regional accents? Unless they are extreme, don't worry about it. It actually adds to your authenticity. I always like to think that my world travels and the fact I speak a second language, Spanish, have resulted in my losing my Philadelphia accent. Not so. My voice shows I am still a Philly guy. If, however, English is your second language, you may wish to enlist the services of an accent reduction coach. They do wonders with foreign-born clients.

Perhaps the main benefit of practicing out loud is that tends to "plant" the words in your brain. You may also discover that that certain words pose a difficulty for you to say. The answer is a thesaurus to find synonyms for words you find difficult to pronounce.

STEP TWO: PRACTICING WITH ONE PERSON

If you have the patience (it can be both boring and frustrating to practice by yourself) go through the solo practice at least three times, reviewing the video after each session. Now invite someone you trust, such as a family member or close friend, to be your audience of one. A spouse can be an excellent one-person audience. Although he or she may not be well-versed in the subject matter of the upcoming presentation, he/she knows you and will be able to see if you are natural or stilted in your delivery.

Additionally, a spouse has a vested economic interest in your success and can serve double duty by operating the video camera or smart phone to do close-ups of your facial expressions.

A colleague from work can also be an excellent sounding board. But another word of caution. Depending on office politics and the competitive environment found in some companies, be careful whom you select. You do not want a person who could benefit by your presenting poorly. A colleague who must also make presentations is a good candidate for he or she realizes that helping you to improve will require you to reciprocate when that person must make a presentation.

Go through this practice presentation with your "audience" from start to finish. If you keep stopping to make corrections, you'll run out of time and your skill level will be uneven. When you have finished this practice session and reviewed your audio- or videotape. You are now ready for your ultimate practice session: **The Murder Board.**

CHAPTER 9

The Murder Board: The Presenter's "Flight Simulator"

THE FLIGHT SIMULATOR enables pilots to learn how to react to in-flight emergencies by simulating them in a safe environment, using sophisticated software and hardware. It is so realistic that pilots have told me they forget where they are, thinking instead that they are in an actual cockpit and about to crash unless they take certain actions immediately. Those actions are what they learn in the flight simulator.

The Murder Board uses a similar method to prepare presenters. It is a rigorous simulation of the presentation to be made, with colleagues role-playing actual audience members, asking the type of questions and raising objections audience members are likely to make. As its macabre name implies, the Murder Board is intended to be more difficult and demanding than the actual presentation.

The Murder Board has it origins in the U.S. Army. It was my "secret sauce" as a speech coach. Very few of my competitors used it or even knew it existed as a teaching method. I wrote several articles on the internet about the Murder Board and they were invariably at the top of Google.

In preparation for writing this chapter I Googled "Murder Board," fully expecting to find my articles at the top. Not so. Those halcyon days are over. In response to a general search my articles have dropped a few pages, replaced by newer articles from various consulting firms.

The sauce is there, but no longer secret, and no longer mine. Most of these newer articles contain a variation on or a verbatim extract of what was in the opening paragraph of all my articles.

Here, for example, is the opening of the article on the Murder Board by the Project Management Institute of Bangalore, India:

> *"The term Murder Board has its origins within the U.S military, specifically in the extensive training system of the U.S. Army. When a person has been selected to be an instructor at an Army school, he or she must go through a special training program."*

I first wrote those words for the Project Management Institute of Washington, DC (PMIWDC). The rest of the Bangalore article is replete with paraphrases and direct quotes from my PMIWDC article, but without attribution. I take consolation, however, in the fact that project managers in India now realize the debt they owe to the United States Army.

Realizing the term had now gone mainstream, I decided to check a reference work I had frequently used: *Safire's Political Dictionary*. The late William Safire was a columnist for the New York Times and had been a presidential speechwriter. He was also the premier "wordsmith" of his time. Sure enough, under "M" I found his coverage of the "Murder Board" where he pointed out that it is used to prepare nominees to the Supreme Court for their confirmation hearings. To my surprise, he closed his passage with these words:

> *"In the article "Internet Marketing and Public Speaking: The Murder Board Practice," Larry Tracy recalled: 'When I ran the Defense Intelligence Agency's (DIA) briefing team, we had three Murder Boards before the daily briefing to the Chairman of the Joint Chiefs of Staff...By the time my briefer or I was standing in front of the Chairman, these intense sessions had provided the*

right answer to virtually any conceivable question the Chairman was likely to ask.' "

I am grateful to the late Mr. Safire for this attribution.

I said in Chapter 8 that I disagreed with fellow speech coaches who put all their emphasis on the solo practice and the practice with an audience of one rather than a full-scale simulated practice session. However, those two steps are certainly valuable prerequisites to having that successful third step, the Murder Board. Before you stand in front of a group of "inquisitors" you want to have converted the written word to the spoken word, have heard your voice and observed your body language by means of a video camera or smart phone.

How a Murder Board is Similar to a Flight Simulator?

Let's return to the first paragraph of this chapter where I described the flight simulator. Ask military or commercial pilots the importance of the "Flight Simulator" and they will tell you tales of how the lessons learned inside that simulated cockpit mounted on a moving platform and with full flight deck instrumentation, taught them how to deal with an in-flight emergency which then saved their lives in an actual emergency at 35,000 feet.

Think back to the "Miracle on the Hudson" in 2009 when USAIR Captain Chesley Sullenberger and his First Officer, Jeff Skiles, successfully "landed" their Airbus 320 on the Hudson River, after birds had disabled the engine. Both pilots had regular sessions in a flight simulator to learn how to react to emergencies, including landing on water. It also helped that Sullenberger was an accomplished glider pilot. I don't want to make too strong a comparison between a Murder Board and a flight simulator because the latter can save lives while the former, merely reputations. What they have in common is the objective of ANTICIPATING problems before they occur.

THE ORIGIN OF THE TERM MURDER BOARD

The first known use of the term in the U.S. Army was in World War II when it was used in the selection process for Officer Candidate School. Over the years it became, as pointed out above, part of the preparation process for instructors in Army schools at Fort Benning, Fort Leavenworth, etc. where designation as instructor is dependent not on passing a written test but instead on successful delivery of a class from the school's curriculum.

Included in the audience for these students are instructors at the school who had already gone through their own Murder Board when they were being prepared to be instructors and are determined that this "newbie" will experience the same frustration and humiliation they had experienced. They ask tough, but realistic, questions. They confront the student instructor with the same pressures and distractions they faced in the classroom. At the end of the simulated class the student instructor gets a "thumbs up," meaning he or she can now join this band of brothers and sisters on the platform, or a "thumbs down," meaning another opportunity to go through a Murder Board.

LESSONS FROM THE PENTAGON

Use of the Murder Board has gone beyond the Army school system and is now used by all the services to prepare those delivering briefings to senior officers. Let me elaborate on the morning routine Mr. Safire described when I headed the Briefing team for the Defense Intelligence Agency.

The first of the three Murder Boards was at 5:30 AM, the second at 6:30 AM and the final practice one hour later. These were all high-pressure sessions with the analysts who had written the items frequently complaining how we had changed their erudite academic analyses into a more cryptic oral presentation which also required graphics to be constantly changed.

The final session began at 7:30 AM in front of an Air Force Major General and a Navy Rear Admiral. It went more smoothly, but once again with more changes. Under the time deadline, both the briefer and the graphics assistant had to be out of the briefing room by 8:20, often on a dead run to reach the Chairman's briefing room. In effect this daily routine was barely- controlled chaos.

THE OBJECTIVE OF THE MURDER BOARD

This rigorous practice session, no less important in a business presentation with millions or perhaps even billions of contract dollars at stake, has three overriding objectives:

1. Honing delivery skills

2. Anticipating probable questions and objections

3. Developing succinct, accurate responses to those questions and objections.

WHY HAVE A MURDER BOARD?

Many presenters, even while accepting the need to sharpen delivery skills, reject the idea of a Murder Board, confident they can anticipate the difficult questions likely to be asked and that they therefore need not perform in front of others, especially their peers. These people may be displaying a false bravado to mask their discomfort at speaking in front of a group.

They are also very mistaken. I have given perhaps 3,000 presentations and always find it beneficial to conduct a Murder Board before an important presentation. The reason we need to test our presentation in front of others is that no matter how hard we try to think of tough questions that may be asked, a little censor in our mind generally provides only questions to which we already have answers. We need other minds to assist us.

The Murder Board is the presenter's equivalent of the actor's dress rehearsal, what lawyers do in preparing a witness to face cross-examination in a trial, and, as I said above, what the flight simulator is to the pilot. Just as with the actor, the witness and the pilot, this simulation permits the presenter to learn from his/her mistakes so that the actual presentation is more responsive to the informational needs of audience members by facilitating the development of answers for questions likely to be asked.

The Murder Board enables you to visualize the presentation in advance. Not only is competence in speaking increased by such a rigorous practice, so is self-confidence. Public speaking ranks high in the pantheon of phobias because of apprehension that one is going to be embarrassed by not being able to answer questions from the audience. If, however, you have been able to anticipate questions, then you can develop answers ahead of time. If still another analogy is needed, think back to when you were in high school, college or graduate school. Your GPA would probably have been higher if you could have seen the questions before the final exams. The Murder Board permits the presenter a legal and ethical look at the audience's "exam questions."

A FINAL WORD ON THE MURDER BOARD

You need to conduct a Murder Board for the same reason that professional football teams go through physically demanding practice sessions before the next game. These athletes and their coaches realize the team will be better prepared by having practiced against what the coaches have anticipated through scouting reports to be the game plan of their upcoming opponent. Presenters must follow the same logic.

It is foolish to deliver a "chips on the line" presentation without going through an intensive Murder Board. The wise presenter realizes that he or she should put as much effort into the presentation as has been put into the product or service being sold. The only obstacle to developing a question-anticipating Murder Board is your imagination and willingness to take hard hits in practice so you can be more effective in the actual presentation.

In Chapter 10 we'll be a bit more granular, enumerating eight steps for a Murder Board that permits you to anticipate questions and objections from your audience.

CHAPTER 10

Eight Steps to a Question–Anticipating Murder Board

To HELP PARTICIPANTS in my workshops internalize how to conduct a successful Murder Board--which will lead to a "buy in"-generating presentation--I teach an eight-step method.

1. How to get colleagues to be on your Murder Board

2. Why you must share with participants intelligence you have on audience members

3. Why your Murder Board participants must role-play the actual audience members

4. The benefits of videotaping and audio taping the Murder Board sessions

5. The need for participants to give honest critiques of your style and substance

6. The need to record all questions asked on 3x5 cards

7. Accept the fact you will likely be required to redo the presentation

8. Do a reverse-role Murder Board: You as audience member, a participant as you.

Let's take a look at each of these steps.

1. How to get colleagues to be on your Murder Board?

In persuading people to be on your Murder Board the best place to start is with knowledgeable colleagues. Request no more than four of these colleagues to be your simulated audience. Keep in mind, however, that if these colleagues think that the objective of the Murder Board is only to help you look good, they probably will not want to give up their valuable time. You must give them an incentive tied to their self-interest.

Frame your request in such a way that these colleagues see a potential dividend accruing to them by investing their time. "What's in it for me?" is the prime motivator for people to take action. You must find a way to have these colleagues believe they will gain by being in your simulated audience. Reciprocity is the key. My advice is to recruit four people who themselves must make presentations. Then you say, "If you will be on my Murder Board now, I will be on yours when you must make a presentation." Presto. They see a potential benefit in the future by spending some time with you now.

Why only four people? One reason is to limit the debts you will have to pay in the future. You do not want to be spending all your available time being on the Murder Boards of others and you certainly do not want to go back on your word.

Another reason is that most audiences you will face have no more than four key people. Having more than four colleagues helping you could result in a less-than-productive bull session, not a question-anticipating Murder Board.

2. SHARE THE INTELLIGENCE YOU HAVE ON AUDIENCE MEMBERS

Because the purpose of a Murder Board is to create an environment for the presenter similar to the actual situation to be faced it is important that those playing the members of the audience be armed with as much information about this audience as possible. That is where the intelligence collection discussed in Chapter 3 comes into play. Participants must be steeped in the details of the issue being presented so they can put themselves in the mental framework of these participants. Information on the personal styles, idiosyncrasies, temperament, etc. of these audience members provides insight into how they will react to certain comments or proposals. Your colleagues can better role-play if they have this information..

If the presentation is to be made internally, say to a Board of Directors or a Committee, participants in this practice session are likely to have valuable information to share with the presenter and other participants. One of the reasons it is beneficial to recruit participants who present regularly is that they may have had the opportunity to present to the same people you are now preparing to address. Colleagues can provide firsthand information on how your actual audience members listen and the kinds of questions they tend to ask.

3. MURDER BOARD PARTICIPANTS ROLE-PLAY THE ACTUAL AUDIENCE MEMBERS

The success or failure of a Murder Board ultimately depends on its realism. The closer it is to the real thing the better prepared will be the presenter. This realism depends on the ability of your colleagues to get into the heads of the key players in your audience.

This does not mean having a great gift for acting or mimicry, but it does mean trying to think like the people in the audience so that statements made by the presenter will provoke questions likely to be asked by the actual audience. After sharing all the intelligence gained on the audience and eliciting from participants any insights they have on these people, assign specific roles to participants. If you are presenting to senior executives, you most certainly want a person to play the key decision-maker.

If the CEO, for example, is an assertive person, try to have an assertive person play this role. If you know that the CEO tends to interrupt presentation with questions, request this role-player to do the same. Remember that role-playing is very dependent on participants having, or having been provided, the most accurate and up-to-date intelligence on this audience.

If they do not have this information, the Murder Board could degenerate into a joking session which may relax you somewhat but will not help you as much as a rigorous, no-holds-barred simulation of that moment of truth when you stand in front of the real audience.

4. BENEFITS OF VIDEOTAPING/ AUDIO TAPING THE MURDER BOARD SESSIONS

The actual conduct of the Murder Board is not likely to run smoothly, but instead be punctuated by various interruptions and discussions. Moreover, the presenter cannot be expected to remember all the comments, bits of advice and questions asked.

Consequently, much of the spontaneous, valuable information could be lost, even if someone is taking careful notes. Consequently, it is beneficial to have both a video camera and an audio recorder running during the practice presentation. This will provide a "game film" enabling you to see and hear yourself as your audience will see and hear you. From the videotape you will learn if you are shifting from one side to the other or grasping the lectern so your knuckles are white from pressure. Only when you see for yourself will you take corrective action.

Having an audio tape of your presentation allows you to focus on those vocal qualities such as monotone, inflection, pitch, speaking rate, "uh's" and "y' knows" discussed in Chapter 14. Because the eye is so powerful you might very well not notice any vocal problems when looking at the videotape. The audiotape will allow you to concentrate on your vocal qualities.

Perhaps the fundamental benefit of recording the practice session is that you will have a record of the questions asked in the give-and-take of the presentation, as well as your answers. Without an electronic record the questions provoked by your presentation and your answers could be lost, thereby negating the benefits of the Murder Board.

5. REQUEST PARTICIPANTS TO GIVE HONEST CRITIQUES OF PERFORMANCE

You have now completed your Murder Board and, in the process, have used the valuable time of your colleagues. Now is the time to ask them for a robust critique of the structure and substance of your presentation and, of course, your delivery style. Keep the video camera and audio recorder rolling. These colleagues may be more expert in certain aspects of your presentation than you are and you certainly want to tap into this expertise.

Additionally, they have just seen you presenting in a stressful environment. Presenting before your colleagues may be more difficult than before a Board of Directors. Consequently, their comments on how you looked, how you sounded and the quality of your overall presence can be invaluable. Thank them for giving up their time and remind them that you are ready to pay back when their time comes to make an important presentation.

You may wish to point out that you have indeed kept within the time limit promised so that you have thereby established a precedent for when your turn comes to be a Murder Board participant.

6. RECORD ALL QUESTIONS ASKED BY PARTICIPANTS ON 3x5 CARDS

You'll need a stack of 3x5 cards. Why? Because you are now going to go through the painful process of listening to how you answered the questions posed by your colleagues. Place each question asked on the front side of a 3x5 card. On the back, in pencil, place the answer you gave or a better one if it occurs to you now…and it probably will. Why pencil? Because you are going to come up with better answers the more you think and research.

When you are at home watching television have that stack of cards nearby. When a commercial comes on the screen, select a card at random, look at the question, give an answer and turn the card over. If your new answer is better than the one on the back of the card, make the correction.

Go through this "flash card" procedure a few times, seeking each time to improve your answer so that you not only address the specifics of the question but also find ways to reinforce your main points. Following this procedure will do much to remove the fear of the unanticipated question, which has such a direct influence on fear of public speaking.

Don't discard the cards after the presentation. They can serve as the foundation for your next presentation. If possible, classify them by subject matter and place them into your database. When you are called on at the last minute to make a short presentation this card file can be a lifesaver and a career-enhancer as you can quickly build a new presentation around one or two old questions.

People will think that you are indeed a silver-tongued orator who can put together a well thought-out and extemporaneous presentation at the last minute. Let them think that. You will know that you are drawing on the "blood, sweat and tears" that went into your Murder Board.

7. YOU WILL LIKELY BE REQUIRED TO REVISE THE PRESENTATION

Having completed your Murder Board you are now faced with a dilemma. What do you do with all the new data generated by this most intense practice session? Remember, your responsibility as a presenter is to provide maximum relevant information in minimum time in the clearest manner possible.

Some of the material you had originally had in your presentation may well have to be dropped, replaced by information that surfaced as a result of questions and discussions in the Murder Board. An approach I have found useful is to time the Murder Board to be somewhat shorter than the time allocated for the actual presentation. This permits a time cushion that allows you to add new material without deleting too much of your original presentation.

It is best to schedule the Murder Board at least two days prior to the actual presentation so you have enough time to revise it to reflect the changes dictated by the questions and comments of your colleagues. This will allow you to integrate the new information and answers that came about as a result of your practice session as well as to develop new visuals, both giving you the opportunity to practice delivering the revised presentation.

8. (OPTIONAL) DO A "REVERSE-ROLE" MURDER BOARD: YOU AS AUDIENCE MEMBER, PARTICIPANT AS YOU

I say "optional" because you may not have the time for this step. I always found it useful to do this "reverse-role Murder Board" perhaps because the different perspective provided by this reversal probably stimulated my brain, allowing me to spot errors in the content or delivery. So, if you have the time, try this. Ask a colleague to learn your presentation and mimic, to the greatest degree possible, your characteristics. He or she should then proceed to deliver your presentation. You take his/her position in the "audience" and listen for how the presentation sounds, if the PowerPoint slides are congruent with the oral message being delivered, and does the presentation you have drafted seem to make sense. Listen as well for how "you" answer questions.

We'll now move on to "show time" with Part Four: "Presenting".

PART FOUR

Presenting

CHAPTER 11

Making "Fear of Speaking" Your Ally

As I pointed out in the Preface, speaking to groups is among the greatest fears in the United States. This was pointed out in the oft-quoted survey of 3,000 Americans published by the <u>Sunday Times of London</u> way back on October 7, 1973. The survey found that 41% of the respondents listed "fear of public speaking" as their number one apprehension while 19% listed "death." This survey was later reported by, and gained notoriety from <u>The Book of Lists.</u> These findings have been verified by countless other surveys and studies. The comedian Jerry Seinfeld joked that this meant most people at a funeral would prefer being in the coffin to delivering the eulogy

Despite the lack of scientific rigor in these surveys, I am inclined to believe them. In the hundreds of workshops I have conducted over the years I have found a high percentage of very intelligent people becoming almost paralyzed at the prospect of delivering a presentation. If you suffer from that same anxiety, rest assured you are in the mainstream of the American public. This chapter will provide some advice on how to make this nervousness work to your advantage.

Many speech coaches believe that one must overcome this fear in order to become an effective speaker. I disagree. As the title of this chapter suggests, I see fear of speaking, the technical name of which is glossophobia, as a great ally for the speaker. Properly controlled, it can provide the adrenalin which leads to enthusiasm. Professional actors are taught to make nervousness work for them, be it in auditions or performances.

Although I have been a "ham" since the first grade when I did my first "show and tell," I normally feel a bit of anxiety when preparing to speak. Certainly when I was facing hostile audiences defending a controversial policy I had the concern of being humiliated.

Once I entered the field of coaching I had less anxiety. After all, I was the "expert." This arrogance changed, however, after delivering a presentation to a convention of commercial real estate brokers. It went well and the audience members were quite enthusiastic about adopting my S3P3 System.

The woman who had hired me made a remark that has had a profound impact on my attitude on coaching. She said, *"You must operate under tremendous pressure when you deliver a presentation."* Considering the audiences I had faced I found her remark puzzling. My arrogant, but unexpressed, thought being "commercial real estate agents causing me pressure after the hostile audiences I had confronted?" I instead responded to her remark by politely asking, *"No, not really, why do you think so?"*

Then came the words that forever changed my approach to coaching. She said, *"Our job is to lease or sell commercial properties which have a market value. If we fail in our presentation, we just do a better job the next time because that property value will not change much. When you make a presentation, however, and it doesn't go well, who will hire you to coach speaking? You are the property and your value will drop with a bad presentation. So I believe you have the pressure of always excelling."* That hit me like punch in the stomach. From that moment on whenever I deliver a presentation or conduct a workshop, before beginning I say the mantra, *"Remember, I am the property!"*

Don't kill the butterflies

Among the physical manifestations of nervousness can be queasiness frequently labeled "butterflies in the stomach." Someone in the field of speech training once said you don't want to kill the butterflies, just get them to fly in formation. Since that original and witty advice was first coined it has had numerous self-described "authors." Most books and workshops on public speaking will offer it as the original insight of the expert who wrote that book or is conducting the workshop.

While I am not claiming credit for that phrase, I certainly agree with its basic premise: that of controlling, not eliminating, nervousness. I always find it disheartening to see or hear colleagues and competitors in the field of presentation skills training promise in their books or workshops that if you only buy their book or attend their workshop, you will never again fear speaking in public.

That is absolute rubbish. It is not only dishonest huckstering, it causes people to make overcoming stage fright their main objective. I have seen many nervous speakers do an outstanding job because they believed in their message and I have seen speakers so calm it seemed rigor mortis had set in. Their calmness made them appear indifferent and they bombed.

You want to be somewhat nervous. It releases the adrenalin that gets you "pumped." That shows passion and enthusiasm. It is the same as the pre–game jitters of athletes which allows them to perform. They are converting nervousness to energy. Presenters must make the same conversion of what is frequently called "stage fright" into positive energy which will demonstrate the presenter's belief in the message.

A TRIO OF FEARS

There are essentially three factors which bring on presentation phobia. I address these in my workshops, showing how to control these fears so they work for, not against, the speaker. Below are those three fears with recommended antidotes.

These remedies have worked for me, they have worked for my workshop participants and they will work for YOU. You'll have those butterflies creating energy, not driving you crazy.

1. FEAR OF THE UNKNOWN

As human beings we tend to be frightened of what we don't know. For presenters the audience is the great unknown. You will wonder, "What do they expect of me? Do they know much more about the subject than I do, etc.?" You will have the tendency to magnify the knowledge of the audience at the expense of your own knowledge.

Antidote: Convert unknown to known.

The more intelligence you gather on the audience and the more intensive your Murder Board, the more the unknown will be converted to known.

Guard against procrastination, however, because we tend to accomplish what is in our comfort zone and put off more difficult tasks such as a systematic Audience Intelligence collection and rigorous practice. Bite the bullet and you will have those fears of the unknown dramatically reduced.

2. FEAR OF FORGETTING

When told they will have to make a presentation many people are consumed by the fear that their mind will go blank and that they will stand in front of the audience without the slightest idea of what they are to say.

They play it safe and write out their presentation then read it verbatim to the audience. This is normally does not turn out well. Audiences want to listen to a speaker who is connecting with them, is looking at them--not at sheets of paper. If you absolutely must read, follow the advice in Chapter 16.

Antidote: The two-card lifesaver.

The reality is that if you have practiced diligently, even a temporary "power outage" of your brain can be handled. The solution I have always used is what I call the two-card lifesaver. Place a startling statistic or interesting fact that you have had to delete for reasons of time on a 3x5 card.

On the second card place a bullet outline of the main points of your presentation. If convenient place these cards in your pocket or on the lectern. If the "My mind has gone blank" syndrome sets in, merely take both cards and say to the audience, "Let me digress for a moment and share with you..." Then relate the information on the first card. If you have prepared well, your mind will probably kick back in and you can continue where you left off. If it does not, slide the second card to the front and look at the bullet points. Select one point and continue the presentation.

Although I always advocate honesty with your audience, I do not recommend that you say, "I forgot what I was going to say." You may get temporary sympathy but then audience members will wonder why they are sitting there if the issue is not important enough for the speaker to remember what he or she was saying.

3. Fear of unanticipated questions

Many people are not unduly worried about making a presentation because they are "on their turf." These same people, however, are terrified at the prospect of answering questions. They believe they will be embarrassed by not being able to answer certain questions. These people are probably perfectionists and believe they must be all-knowing of all things.

Antidote: Anticipate the questions.

I realize that may sound simplistic, inviting the response, "Yeah, right." Remember, however, that learning what audience members will ask is precisely the goal of the Murder Board which was extensively covered in Chapters 9 and 10.

If you have acquired accurate intelligence on the audience's needs, concerns and problems, as shown in Chapter 3, then you should be able to preempt certain questions, and anticipate others. There's a certain pleasure when you "hold a zinger" in reserve. This is where the Murder Board is invaluable.

For perfectionists who think they must be able to answer every question, chill out. No one expects you to have all the information, but they do expect you to be honest. Don't give a false answer just to avoid the embarrassment of admitting, "I don't know." That phrase, followed by "but I'll get that information for you," should be in every presenter's vocabulary. When you make that commitment remember that you have a moral obligation to follow up and provide the answer, through some means, to the questioner… and perhaps to the entire audience.

In Chapter 12, we'll look at the three intangibles of Credibility, Clarity and Conviction which are absolutely vital for every presenter.

CHAPTER 12

The Three "C's": Credibility, Clarity and Conviction

COULD HAVE FOLDED this material into another chapter but decided it deserved to stand alone so you will grasp the importance of the "Three "C's." Even if you have planned and practiced as I recommend, but lack these intangibles, you will not get "buy-in" from audience members. The Three C's are that vital.

Let's take a look at them:

CREDIBILITY

In *The Rhetoric*, Aristotle wrote 2,500 years ago that there were three means of persuasion: *Ethos, Pathos* and *Logos*. The first referred to the speaker's perceived character, including honesty; the second to emotional appeals by the speaker; and the third the intellectual content of the message. Ethos, what we today call credibility, was regarded by Aristotle as the most important of the three. He maintained that if the audience knew nothing of the subject but believed the speaker was honest, had integrity and possessed knowledge of the issue, they would accept the message which was being delivered. With credibility a speaker has a chance of bringing an audience to his/her side. Without it the speaker is dead in the water.

Shortly after I entered the field of speech coaching, I wrote an article in "Training and Development Magazine," the official publication of the American Society for Training and Development titled, *"Taming Hostile Audiences Persuading Those Who Would Rather Jeer than Cheer."* (It is Appendix 1 of this book.) I listed the components of credibility as Expertise, Believability and Likeability, in that order. Over the many years since I wrote the article my views have evolved. I now would place Likeability ahead of the other two. Why? Because if audience members don't like you, your expertise and believability will not count. They will just ignore what you have to say.

Humans have a tendency to accept information from people they like, as opposed to those who cause the temperature in the room to drop when they walk in. If you have an aloof attitude, little expression in your voice and facial expression, you must strive to improve on these aspects. If someone who works for you has such problem, have them develop the warmer aspects of their personality.

After Likeablity comes the speaker's demonstrated Knowledge of the issue being discussed and appreciation of the problems of the audience members. They will ask, "Can this speaker show that he or she can apply his/her knowledge to my problems?" All audiences are self-centered. In listening to a presentation, members are asking, "What's in it for me?"

Finally, is the speaker Believable or so glib and smooth that audience members wonder if they are listening to an actor? There must be an authenticity to the speaker. This can be demonstrated by tone of voice, eye contact, a genuine concern for audience members. True, a skilled actor may be able to fool audience members but this is not likely in most presentations.

Here is the key takeaway on credibility. IT IS SUBJECTIVE. The audience will determine whether or not the speaker has credibility. None of you reading this, nor I, can say, "I have credibility to speak (or write) on this subject." That's why I placed testimonials of my speaking and coaching at the front of this book: to help you decide if I had the background to help you improve your speaking skills. Human beings are looking for "social proof" before they make the decision to buy a product or accept a position being advocated. To present your credentials to an audience, have someone else introduce you. A phrase that makes me cringe is when I when I hear a speaker say, "Let me tell you about myself." Ugh!

CLARITY

It certainly seems obvious that a presentation must be clearly stated. Ideally, we would like to have 100% congruence between what the speaker says and what audience members hear. That, however, is impossible. We speak, and we listen through the prisms of our own experiences. Added to obstacles preventing clear communication of ideas is the fact that now in the United States we live in such a multi-cultural, multi-lingual society that we can never be sure that audience members for whom English is a second language will understand what we are saying. So intelligence-gathering on audience members, discussed in Chapter 3, must include this component.

In my workshops I frequently tell participants to think of a presentation as being four presentations, to make them realize the challenge they face in seeking clarity of expression.

1. THE PRESENTATION YOU PLAN TO DELIVER

We all plan, to a greater or lesser extent, what we are going to say in a presentation. It may be just to inform or it may be to cause the audience to change direction. It should, of course, be oriented to solving audience member's problems. In theory we are "game planning" the presentation. How close the actual presentation is to how we planned it to be depends on how detailed was our planning.

2. THE PRESENTATION YOU ACTUALLY DELIVER

In most cases our actual presentations are considerably different than how we thought they would be. Questions are asked and objections made that we had not anticipated. Nervousness can throw us off as well. You may also have miscalculated how much time you had for the presentation. Why is there such a difference between what you planned and what you actually presented? Perhaps because your planning was insufficient. Of course, you can close the gap between what you planned to say and what you actually say by writing and delivering your remarks verbatim. But then you would be so boring that your audience would not be listening.

3. THE PRESENTATION YOU WISH YOU HAD DELIVERED

When your actual presentation falls short of what you had hoped to accomplish, you experience what may be called "presenter's remorse." You know you should have had greater congruence between how you planned and how you delivered. This can now be a teaching moment. Having been disappointed in the outcome, you now can see how you should have prepared. Your goal is now to factor in the lessons learned, so you can, in the next presentation, make the actual presentation closer to what you had planned.

4. THE PRESENTATION YOUR AUDIENCE ACTUALLY HEARS

Unfortunately, few audiences pay attention 100% of the time and there are many distractions that get in the way of audience comprehension of the message of a speaker. Audience members are probably checking their e-mail, thinking of appointments they have, ruminating about personal or professional problems, etc. Additionally, as I said above, in our multi-cultural, multi-language society, many audience members will have learned English as a second language. A speaker must be aware of these problems.

Perhaps the best definition I have seen of a speaker's "clarity" comes from the 19th Century philosopher, Ralph Waldo Emerson, who wrote:

"Clarity is the power to translate a truth into terms perfectly intelligible to the person being spoken to."

Remember this. Clarity is 100% the responsibility of the speaker. No speaker can say, "I was clear, but they didn't get it." If "they" didn't get it, it is the speaker's fault.

CONVICTION

The speaker looking to to cause audience members to "buy in" to what he or she is advocating must speak with passion and conviction. If the speaker does not seem enthused on the issue, why should audience members? This does not mean that you must jump around like a televangelist but it does mean that you should show a intense belief in what you are saying.

To be convincing a presenter must exude confidence and this can best be achieved by going through several Murder Boards. Essentially, the presenter by showing confidence (not arrogance) can cause audience members to give him or her a chance to make his or her case.

There is a valid scientific reason why audience members can be convinced not just by the intellectual content of the message, but also by the way the message is delivered. In Chapter 14, I discuss how in the 1990s, Italian researchers discovered an element in the brain which they dubbed the "mirror neuron." They saw lab monkeys mimicking gestures of their human handlers. When electrodes were attached to the brains of the monkeys the scientists observed that this part of the brain would light up when the monkey grabbed an object. It would likewise light up when the monkey saw the human handler grab the same object.

This phenomenon been adapted to sales training. Various experiments have shown that when a sales person "mirrors" the gestures, vocal modulation and mannerisms of the prospective client, the salesperson has a greater likelihood of making the sale. For speakers the "mirror neuron" can prove to be a great advantage. Audience members observing a speaker who is passionate about the point he or she is advocating are likely to experience this same passion. I'll have much more to say about this fascinating discovery of how the brain influences behavior in Chapter 14 on Non-Verbals.

In Chapter 13, I'll take great pleasure in demolishing one of the great myths in speech coaching: the one that says only 7% of a message received by audience members is imparted by the spoken word whereas 93% is from body language and vocal quality of the presenter. If that seems idiotic to you, read on.

CHAPTER 13

NON-VERBALS 1: Destroying the Mehrabian Myth

F OR THOSE OF you who have read other books on public speaking, the numbers 55, 38 and 7 may ring a bell. Or perhaps the name Dr. Albert Mehrabian, Professor Emeritus of Psychology at the University of California at Los Angeles (UCLA), will seem familiar. Let me explain.

When I entered the field of speech coaching I wanted to become familiar with the literature of the field and started reading books about presentation skills. I was surprised to find in many of them the view that how you looked and sounded was more important than what you said. To back up this assertion these authors quoted from Dr. Mehrabian's 1972 book, *Silent Messages: Implicit Communication of Emotions and Messages.* The typical remark in these books was that 7% of a message is verbally communicated, 55% is communicated through body language--primarily facial expression-- and 38% through vocal tonality.

I found this utter nonsense based on my experience of delivering some 3,000 presentations. To me it means that a person who was Hollywood handsome/beautiful and spoke with a pleasing, mellifluous voice, could utter absolute gibberish and receive a "grade" of 93%! I bought a copy of *Silent Messages* and located the paragraph where Dr.

Mehrabian showed the results of his study. I noted he did not refer to "communication" but instead to "liking".

In my workshops I made reference to the Mehrabian study as one where there had been great misinterpretation. I believed that communication was a blending of intellectual content and non-verbal delivery modes: gestures, facial expression and vocal quality. I even designed a PowerPoint slide showing a message as a missile, with the first stage being body language/facial expression and the second stage being vocal quality. The "payload" was the message content.

Speech coaches who took the "93%" position had obviously, intentionally or not, misinterpreted Dr. Mehrabian's research. I concluded they did so to impress their clients/readers with the importance of style--their strong point--over substance, the strong point of their clients. A person I knew (whom I will not mention to avoid embarrassing him) even wrote a book based on the "Mehrabian Law."

A few years ago, when my wife and I were visiting our daughter and family in London, I visited a book store and, as was my habit, went to the section on presentation skills and browsed the index of each book. I searched for "Mehrabian" or "55-38-7." Invariably I'd find the author praising this "breakthrough" study. I would put the book back on the shelf, believing it was not worth reading.

Then I came upon a book, titled *Lend me Your Ears,* by Professor Max Atkinson. In the index I found "Mehrabian, Albert, misinterpretation of his findings, 342-5." My eyes lit up. Had I found a kindred spirit? On page 342 Professor Atkinson, whom I subsequently learned was one of the top presentation skills coaches in England, skewered the advocates of the 93% school of thinking, pointing out how this theory went against common sense. He wrote:

> " *Perhaps the most damaging feature of these claims is that they help to spread and consolidate the myth that non-verbal behavior is so overwhelmingly dominant that the words we use to convey our message are of little or no importance. This is not only grossly misleading, but also increases the normal anxieties of*

*speech-making with a catalogue of extra things to worry about,
such as stance, gesture and movement."*

He then backed up his assertion by showing he had done something
I should have done: He reached out to Dr. Mehrabian at UCLA, asking
him his view of how "experts" had reported his findings. Dr. Mehrabian
responded that his original work had, as I said above, concentrated on
people "liking" each other.

Dr. Mehrabian went on to say:

*"I am obviously uncomfortable about misquotes of my work.
From the very beginning, I have tried to give people the correct
limitations of my findings. Unfortunately, the field of self-styled
"corporate image consultants" or "leadership consultants" has
numerous practitioners" with very little psychological expertise."*

As I was writing this chapter, on a whim I Googled "The Mehrabian
Myth." To my surprise, I found several articles debunking the "93%"
theory. They point out the same arguments which Professor Atkinson
and I have made, but they do not cite the most powerful witness of all:
Dr. Mehrabian. So I am happy to have corrected, along with Professor
Atkinson, the record. Dr. Mehrabian's reputation has been sullied by
speech coaches who have misinterpreted and misquoted an honorable
scholar.

In Chapter 14 we'll look in detail at how non-verbals can have both
a negative and positive impact on presentations, and explore in more
depth that a unique element of the human brain: "Mirror Neurons."

CHAPTER 14

NON-VERBALS 2: Dress, Body, Voice and the Mirror Neuron

A PRESENTATION IS MORE than the sum of the words spoken. The perception by audience members of how the speaker looks and sounds has a decided impact, both positive and negative, on how the message is accepted. A trite but true adage is "You cannot not communicate."

In this chapter I want to show how appearance, voice and body language influence audience members. Despite what we would like to think--that it is the lucidity of our argument that persuades an audience to our point of view --empirical research on group behavior suggests strongly that non-verbal communication has a significant impact on how these audience members interpret our presentation.

When you have an important message don't shoot yourself in the foot by delivering it with flawed, non-verbal communication. A message vital to audience members but delivered in a boring monotone, perhaps being read from a text or words on a screen, can easily turn off these people. There is little doubt that a degree of acting and stagecraft are a part of even the most serious presentation.

Here are some tips to assist you in being "non-verbally fluent."

The "first impression" factor

The audience will make an immediate judgment about you by your clothing and grooming. You do not want the audience's memory of how you dressed to overshadow the intellectual content of your presentation.

Advice for men

Generally speaking, men do not have as good a sense of style and color coordination as do women. Dark suits are better than light (although in the summer light-colored suits are acceptable). Neatly pressed white shirts are advisable. Ties should be conservative, as you never wish to have audience members distracted by overly "flashy" neckwear. The traditional red "power tie" is always a good bet. Keep your suit coat buttoned and your tie centered. The buttoned coat shows respect for your audience. The open coat is can be interpreted by some audience members as connoting a casual approach to an issue they take seriously. A tie that is off-center can be very distracting, not just for "neat freaks" in the audience. Shoes should match the suit (no brown shoes with a dark suit), they should not be run-down at the heels and should be shined.

If you are presenting to a business group, members of this audience are not expecting you to make a fashion statement. They are expecting you to dress in a conservative manner consistent with the message you are delivering and the nature of this audience. A useful rule of thumb is dress one step up from the audience. If they are in sport coats, wear a suit. If they are in very casual attire, wear a sport coat.

Advice for women

Women have much more flexibility than do men and can dress conservatively yet stylishly. My advice is to not wear excessive jewelry that may be distracting or noisy. Earrings that are very large and/or which reflect the light can distract. Avoid bracelets which can jingle or make thumping sounds into the microphone. If you are speaking from a raised platform, skirt length can also be distracting. Conservative but not dowdy is best.

Women tend to wear shoes that are in vogue even if they are not comfortable. Ill-fitting high heel shoes-however beautiful and stylish-can prove very painful, even dangerous, to the woman presenter who is on her feet for a lengthy presentation and question-and-answer session.

BODY LANGUAGE

Studies indicate that when people detect a difference between the non-verbal body language and the spoken language they tend to believe the non-verbal. A speaker saying, "I'm very happy to be with you," while wringing his or her hands might not be considered a happy camper. Hand-wringing and other non-verbal flaws may also be perceived by the audience as nervousness which has been generated by delivering a message that is not true, even if it is.

AVOIDING "HAPPY FEET"

A stressful situation, such as speaking before a group, activates adrenaline. This can manifest itself in pacing back and forth. While it is best to have movement, rather than appear like a statue, make this movement with a purpose. If not tied to a lectern, move toward the audience and then back up, never turning your back on the group. (Professional actors are taught never to turn their backs on the audience because it severs their connection with the audience!) Be aware, of course, of any furniture that could painfully interrupt your backward movement.

GESTURES

Movement of the hands and arms should be natural and energetic but not so expansive as to make you appear to be a televangelist who has had too much coffee. The hands and arms can serve as visual exclamation points for your words. Just don't overdo them because you are not playing Hamlet when making a presentation. Imagine you are speaking to a friend on your cellular phone. Gestures can reduce a monotone. It is almost impossible to speak in boring tones when gesturing and it is very difficult to avoid a monotone when your arms are at your side.

EYE CONTACT

Americans are distrustful of a person who does not look them in the eyes. Good eye contact helps a speaker reach out to an audience and establish the human contact which is so much a part of the oral presentation. Pick a person (preferably friendly) in each section of the room and rotate your gaze around the room by having a brief "conversation" (no more than two sentences) with that person.

This will help you to connect with the audience, and it will calm your nerves. However, when giving a presentation to, say, the CEO of a company, devote most of the eye contact time to this person, breaking contact periodically to look at other people, giving that senior person a rest from intensive eye contact with you, the presenter.

FACIAL EXPRESSION

Audience members will be looking at your face when you speak. They will instinctively note any discrepancy between the message you are conveying and the expression on your face. Again, the speaker saying how happy he or she is to be speaking but who accompanies this message with a poker face and a monotone is inviting skepticism. If you are providing bad news, but doing so with a smile, audience members will detect a mixed message. Congruency between message, body language and facial expression goes a long way toward establishing credibility.

THE VOICE

The voice does the heavy lifting in any presentation. Some people are blessed with mellifluous voices which are so pleasing to the ear that audiences may not even pay attention to the thoughts being expressed.

Many of us must actively guard against the problems of accents, problems associated with tone and pitch, a too fast or too slow rate of delivery, speaking too loudly or (more commonly) too softly. Then, of course, there is the bane of all speakers: the use of those abominable fillers, "uh" and "y'know".

Below are some of the most common vocal problems along with advice on how to correct them.

REGIONAL ACCENT

Accents in the United States frequently cause more concern among self-conscious presenters than it does with audiences listening to them. Many presenters feel an undeserved sense of inferiority if their accent is distinctly different from the accents of those to whom they are speaking. You should, of course, be careful about your diction and pronunciation, but realize that television has brought all kinds of accents into our homes and audiences are accepting of these differences. Still, the closer you can come to mainstream English--perhaps like that of a television newsreader--the better off you will be.

FOREIGN ACCENT

Americans as a rule do not have a good ear for foreign accents. This can cause problems for the non-native speaker of English. If he or she has a strong accent, their American audiences may not understand essential parts of the presentation. If audience members cannot understand what the presenter is saying, the message will not be conveyed. An accent reduction coach should be consulted.

TONE

Men have a tendency to speak in a monotone, which can be very annoying and boring. If you have this problem, practice speaking with an audio recorder, placing emphasis on verbs and other words which connote action and movement. Underlining or printing these words in bold type can assist in overcoming this mannerism. Women generally do not have the monotone problem as they generally speak with inflection.

Pitch

Too high a pitch can be irritating to the human ear. Women presenters-and some men-might do well to lower their pitch. Most women on television speak within the comfort range of the human ear.

Rate of delivery

A good rate of delivery is approximately 150 words per minute but even this should be varied. The delivery rate should also be adapted to the audience. A group in New York would be irritated by slow delivery while an audience in Dallas would be put off by a machine-gun delivery. I know. When I was speaking in that city one time an irritated member of the audience shouted, "Slow down, Yankee!" I did.

Volume

Although some men speak at too low a volume, it is more a problem for women. To develop higher volume ask a colleague to stand in the back of a large room, such as an auditorium, holding his or her arm at waist level. As you speak, the colleague then raises that arm until you reach the level at which the colleague can comfortably hear you. Maintain that volume and you will now know at what level you should speak.

"Uh's" and "Y'knows"

These sounds, which in a perfect world would be expunged from our oral vocabulary, can destroy an otherwise well-crafted presentation. There are variants to these utterances, but concentrating on eliminating them would be a good start to becoming a better speaker. Audience members are sensitive to these sounds and might start counting how many times the presenter uses them. When attention is focused on counting, little attention can be devoted to absorbing the substance of the presentation.

A drill to help you reduce "uh's" and "y'knows" in your delivery is to have colleagues in a practice session shout "Uh!" when you utter that sound, and "No, we don't!" when you say "Y'know." I use this exercise in my workshops and it works wonders. People must be aware that they are using these sounds before they can take steps to reduce their use.

Mirror Neurons

As a speaker and speech coach I have always been fascinated with how the brain processes information, how a firmly held view of audience members can be altered by the words of a presenter. The most inclusive, easiest-to-understand book I read on how our grey matter functions was "The Brain" by Dr. Richard Restak. At the end of this chapter I'll reveal how I embarrassed myself when I had a chance meeting with Dr. Restak.

For now we'll discuss how peanut-loving monkeys in Italy caused the discovery of "mirror neurons" which had far-reaching implications for how the brain functions. In 1995 neuroscientists at Parma University in Italy were studying the brains of monkeys to see how these simians reacted to certain stimuli--in this case eating peanuts. From that rather inauspicious beginning came a profound finding about how the human brain reads other human brains, how one person's emotions affect another person's, how empathy develops. For speakers, mirror neurons can be a powerful tool in the non-verbal toolbox.

The researchers noticed how a particular area of the monkey's brain would light up on eating a peanut. When one of the researchers ate the peanut himself, rather than giving it to the monkey, the same pleasure area of the monkey's brain lit up, apparently signaling that the monkey was "mirroring" the pleasure of the peanut-eating researcher. This led to further investigation and the discovery that monkeys and humans have elements of the brain, which the researchers dubbed mirror neurons, that reflect and mimic the actions of others. This has had profound implications in brain research, including a scientific explanation for empathy: how we relate to other people. Let me give you a recent personal experience to illustrate this fact.

During the final stages of writing this book I attended a networking breakfast. As I was leaving, deep in thought as to how to conclude this chapter on non-verbals, I was not paying attention to where I was walking. I stepped on a curb, not noticing that it was separated from the pavement not by grass but instead by rocks which were about an inch higher than the curb and pavement. I failed to lift my foot, which hit the rocks, and down I went, headfirst. I saw blood dripping on the rocks as people from the breakfast called 911 and also applied towels to stop the bleeding. If you are beginning to experience my pain it's because your mirror neurons are firing. I was taken to a hospital. The wound was closed with five stitches and covered by a large bandage. I also had a badly bruised nose and my left hand was badly cut. I was a mess.

When I came home and saw a neighbor she asked, "What happened to you?" I recounted the events of the morning and noticed she was grimacing as if she had fallen. Her mirror neurons were firing. I decided to do a further experiment. The next neighbor I saw asked the same question. This time I was a bit more dramatic with my words. I recounted how I had "smashed" my head on rocks and the blood was "pouring out" before I was "rushed" by ambulance to the Emergency Room. This fellow was now grimacing as if he had hit his head on the rocks. He was indeed feeling my pain.

You are probably wondering how peanut-loving monkeys in Italy have anything to do with non-verbals for presenters. Quite a bit, actually, and I'm surprised all speech coaches do not include this in their coaching. To the best of my knowledge the only other one who does is Nick Morgan of Harvard, an excellent coach and prolific writer. His book, "Power Cues," which I have drawn on here, does a deep dive into the subject and I recommend you read it. Another excellent book I recommend which treats mirror neurons in great detail is "Instant Appeal" by Vicki Kunkel.

As both of these authorities point out, an effective persuasive presentation is based on relations between the persuader and the "persuadees."

As presenters we must attempt to read the minds of audience members. They in turn are reading ours, attempting to determine if we are honest or mere "spinmeisters." This mutual reading has existed for eons but not until 1995 did we have a scientific basis for understanding the process. Nick Morgan quotes the lead neuroscientist from Parma University, Giacomo Rizzolatti, explaining:

> *" The mirror neuron systems…provided us with a base from which to investigate the cerebral processes responsible for the vast range of behaviours that characterize our daily existence, and from which we weave the web of our social and inter-individual relations. When we are delivering a presentation which has as its purpose causing listeners to change their mind, we must be able (and willing) to accept elements of an opposing position held by members of the audience, as we hope that the principle of reciprocity will come into play and these listeners will accept elements of our position. That is bringing us to a middle ground from which we can hopefully move them to our position. If these audience members remain intransigent, there is little chance of them "buying."*

What came to be named "mirror neurons" has, of course, existed and evolved in the human brain for eons. When I was preparing to address audiences opposed to the policy I was advocating, I was seeking to lower their hostility by having a positive impression of me. I knew if I had any chance of bringing members of an audience to accept my message, they had to have a positive impression of the me, the messenger. This was just common sense.

I mentioned in Chapter 3 the importance of gaining Micro-Intelligence on audience members and how I used the "beer-and-pizza" method to establish rapport with leaders of a student group strongly opposed to US policy. I didn't know it at the time (the peanut-eating monkeys in Italy had not yet led to that monumental discovery) but I was striving to get the students' "mirror neurons" firing on my behalf. It was a tactic I used many times when speaking at colleges.

How the brains of audience members process the information being presented by speakers is key to how we can "bring home the bacon." How you use gesture, your tone of voice, your acceptance of positions of the audience can all create a positive impression of you, the presenter, and of information which audience members will agree with. In Chapter 15 we'll discuss a related element of presenter-audience relations: Cognitive Dissonance.

At the outset of this chapter I mentioned my admiration for the book, "The Brain" by Richard Restak MD., Ph.D. who is a neurologist, neuropsychiatrist and professor of Clinical Psychology at the George Washington University School of Medicine. Several years ago my wife and I attended a noisy cocktail party in Washington, DC. I found myself speaking to a person whom I did not know, and did not catch his name, and somehow the conversation drifted to how we process information. Having recently read "The Brain," I wanted to help this person increase his wisdom, so I recommended he read the book by Dr. Richard Restak. The gentleman smiled and said "I am Richard Restak."

Lesson learned? Get the name of the person you are trying to impress.

CHAPTER 15

Turning Cognitive Dissonance to Your Advantage

N 1957 THE late social psychologist, Leon Festinger, Ph.D., wrote what was destined to become a landmark book on how people process information. In <u>A Theory of Cognitive Dissonance</u> Festinger revealed the results of studies he conducted to measure whether people readily changed their minds when presented with new information that contradicted views they already held. Did they analyze the new data, compare it with the information already possessed and then arrive at a new conclusion through a rational reasoning process? Or did they stubbornly cling to their existing belief despite the evidence presented to support the new but contradictory information? What he found was surprising and controversial. Thousands of similar studies, however, have shown Festinger's findings to be valid.

THE FESTINGER EXPERIMENTS

Dr. Festinger concluded that the human mind is not comfortable accommodating two contradictory notions simultaneously. People want a consistent relationship between their values/beliefs and their actions. When this lack of consistency is present--dissonance in Festinger's terminology-- people become uncomfortable and seek to regain the equilibrium between beliefs and actions. They wish to reduce the dissonance, and, in the case of an audience listening to a presentation at variance with their existing beliefs, they seek to reduce this dissonance by either (1) rejecting the new information or (2) accepting it and changing their view to one more consistent with the new information.

He also discovered that when new information is introduced which contradicts existing attitudes, many people, rather than initiating a rational recalculation, will reject that new information. In effect the mind wants harmony and does not want dissonance, or disharmony. One of Festinger's experiments demonstrated this when he asked participants whether they thought cheating on an examination was always wrong or if there were situations in which cheating was justified. He then set up a scenario in which participants were asked to take an examination in which achieving a certain grade would prove beneficial for those participants. A number of subjects who had voiced strong moral opposition to cheating were in fact observed looking at the papers of classmates and subsequently, when questioned about the morality of cheating on an examination, expressed a more ambiguous position. They were obviously seeking to justify their actions by changing their beliefs.

HOW WE HANDLE DISSONANCE

We become comfortable with a judgment, opinion, or belief and are reluctant to accommodate new information that causes us to change our judgment, opinion or belief. By changing our mind we are admitting we had not made a wise choice initially, that we had done insufficient research on the matter. Curiously, in the case of actions that people performed which tended to counter what they thought were their values and beliefs, they sometimes tended to change these beliefs, thereby rationalizing their actions.

How Presenters Can Turn Cognitive Dissonance to Their Advantage

For a presenter cognitive dissonance is a double-edged sword. If members of the audience are being introduced to information at variance with their beliefs, these people are likely to resist accepting the speaker's message. They will protect their opinions, despite the lucidity of arguments to the contrary. This can make it difficult to reach such people who are intransigent. The other side of the sword, however, creates an opportunity for the speaker who can show that he or she is a reasonable, open-minded person, whose values, if not opinions, are similar to those in the audience opposed to the position being advocated.

This can create a degree of cognitive dissonance in certain audience members. They may become uncomfortable with the information they brought to the presentation. They like and respect the messenger and wonder how they can be in disagreement with the point being advocated by a person so similar to them. The presenter who can create cognitive dissonance does so because he or she realizes that facts alone do not persuade. Such a presenter has learned to appeal to the emotional and psychological side of the audience. When you are confronted with an audience appearing to have a high degree of cognitive dissonance, let these people save face by having the new information presented in such a manner that they can avoid being forced to admit to themselves and others that they were wrong.

A speaker representing an organization may accept responsibility for not having provided the new information earlier, thus leading audience members to say to themselves, "Had I known that information I would naturally have come to a different conclusion than I did. Now, with this new data, I will use reason and change my mind."

In Chapter 16, I'll show how to minimize the problems created when you are required to read your presentation.

CHAPTER 16

When You Must Read

L ET ME START with a bias I believe is shared by many. I have an intense dislike of listening to a speech or presentation that is read. My immediate reactions are to:

1. Wonder who actually wrote the speech;

2. Prefer being given a copy to read at my leisure;

3. Become bored and inattentive as the speaker drones on.

Having gotten that off my chest I'll now say that there are times when a speaker has no alternative--he or she must read the speech. That is the sour lemon we must all accept from time to time. In this chapter I'll show you how to make lemonade. (Not very original, I admit, but it does fit.)

WHEN IS READING NECESSARY

When the President of the United States speaks from the Oval Office or delivers a State of the Union address, his words have been crafted and vetted carefully. A casual ad-lib or personal aside could have international ramifications. On these occasions, of course, the President is reading from a teleprompter but the television audience has the feeling he is speaking extemporaneously to them. Some other instances require reading such as:

1. When the Chairman of the Federal Reserve speaks on the economy these words are likewise carefully chosen and delivered verbatim lest there be a global stock market crash.

2. A newsreader on television or radio is under severe time limits and must read from a teleprompter or script.

3. Time constraints for business presentations are a factor that could ultimately cause a presentation to be read, as could a situation where the scheduled presenter is indisposed and a last minute substitute must step in.

4. When you are told by your boss that these are the "golden words" and no deviation is permitted.

WHY MANY PRESENTERS CHOOSE TO READ

Many presenters, unfortunately, choose to read their presentation even when it is not required. For the most part, they do so because of their fear of speaking. They are afraid they will forget what they were going to say. Having a written text in front of them is a security blanket. Anecdotes abound about corporate CEOs and politicians who read their speechwriter-prepared presentations, only to stumble through words with which they were not familiar or in some other way provided comic relief to their audiences. Their problem, of course, was that they were not trying to be funny.

They walked to the lectern, kept their eyes on the text, and never saw the audience until finished. The following true story is frequently told in Washington. A Senator (who shall remain anonymous) was handed his speech by a staff member just before ascending the podium. Unfortunately for the Senator, he failed to note that the first page was the press release touting how his remarks were greeted with thunderous applause. The hapless Senator read the press release, to the dismay of his staff, as his audience roared with laughter.

I'm going to provide two solutions you can use when you are either tempted or directed to read verbatim from a script. You'll find that these alternatives will enable you to have a "crutch" without boring your audience. For those who are directed to follow a corporate line, either of these solutions will get you off the hook. I've used both solutions myself and they work.

SOLUTION ONE: DOCTOR THE SCRIPT

If you are preparing to deliver a written report orally, you are not necessarily in a no-win situation. You can rewrite it to put the written information into spoken language. (This is another justification as to why your speech should be double-spaced: to give you room for corrections, sometimes on the fly at the lectern.) Changing how the words appear on your script can help you sound more natural, sincere and spontaneous.

If you cannot alter the words, alter the formatting. A written report is quite naturally written for the eye--the way we are accustomed to writing, single space and in 12-point font. If, however, you change the formatting, a more natural delivery will ensue. Your eye contact with the audience will improve and you will sound more conversational yet you are still delivering the words the audience must hear. You'll find that this requires a good bit of pre–presentation work on your part, but the payoff is that you'll look more in command and less of a robot who is reading words written by another person.

Here are some ways to doctor any script. I found them useful when I had to read words that had been "blessed" by a higher authority. They are purely mechanical and do not alter those words which have been mandated by your superiors. A memo or speech written in conventional 12-point font will cause numerous blunders when you have to read it from the lectern. The stress of speaking will affect your reading ability and the lighting at the lectern may make reading difficult.

My advice is to use 24-point font, bold type and double spacing. Scripts for voiceover artists (actors who do radio commercials and narrations) are typed in very large font and double-spaced so that errors by the copywriter can be addressed and so that any last-minute changes ordered by the account executive or producer can be written in by the actor who then modifies his or her delivery. You may think that 24-point is too large a font. When you stand at a lectern with a dim light that may reflect from the paper into your eyes you'll be glad you have large print to read. Use upper- and lowercase type. Some believe that typing in all capital letters will make it easier to read. Not so. We are accustomed to reading in lower case. However, the scripts for voiceover artists, who are professionals as opposed to us, are almost always written in all capital letters.

Wide margins, short paragraphs, bottom third blank. Complement the 24- point font with wide margins so that your eyes need not travel from left to right on the page. When possible, create paragraphs of no more than six lines. Coupled with the six words across resulting from the large font, you will be able to take in the words without moving your eyes from left to right. The paragraph breaks will enable you to have more eye contact with the audience. Large margins will provide space for notes on both sides of the text that cue you when to pause, when to look at the audience, and so on.

Leave the bottom third of the page blank, so you will not be required to lower your head too much. That will also facilitate having more eye contact with audience members. Underline, highlight or make the type bold for emphasis. When you speak extemporaneously or conversationally you will be more inclined to use natural inflection. When reading you are likely to read aloud the way you read silently--in a monotone.

To avoid doing this underline key words and phrases requiring emphasis with a highlighter or use bold type. Practice with and audio recorder or video camera. Read through the entire presentation, then listen to yourself. You want to sound enthused and passionate about your subject. Above all you want to avoid the droning on in a monotone: the fundamental complaint of audiences forced to endure a presentation that is read from a script.

SOLUTION TWO: PROVIDE THE SCRIPT IN ADVANCE, THEN GO TO Q & A

A far less complicated alternative is to have the presentation prepared for the eye (12-point font, one-inch margins) as a monograph, which you then provide to all audience members. Deliver a brief, extemporaneous oral executive summary then open for questions-and-answers. By doing this, you have the best of both worlds. You comply with the requirement to provide the audience with the blessed words, but you avoid boring them to death.

Whether you choose solution one or solution two you will be far better off than if you read in what will probably inevitably degenerate into a boring monotone. And your audience will appreciate it.

In Chapter 17, I'll show how employing certain rhetorical devices can make you appear a more experienced, polished speaker than may be the case.

CHAPTER 17

Shortcuts to Eloquence

Y<small>OU HAVE PROBABLY</small> had the experience of listening to a speaker who, even if you did not agree with that person's message, caused you to think, "This is an outstanding speaker!" That speaker was probably using certain phrases that touched an internal chord.

Normally such techniques are used by experienced speakers who have honed them over time. Yet you do not need to have delivered hundreds of presentations to develop the ability to incorporate techniques which add grace, forcefulness and vividness to your presentation.

WHAT IS ELOQUENCE?

To speak eloquently does not mean speaking in polysyllabic phrases aimed less at communicating than impressing. Truly eloquent speakers use short, direct, specific language aimed at their listeners. Winston Churchill's stirring speeches during World War II are prime examples of such language. Eloquent speakers, like Churchill and John F. Kennedy, realize that the spoken word must appeal to the ear more than the eye and that nothing appeals more than repetition, rhythm and cadence.

Cadence is the rhythmic beat of spoken words. The eloquent presentation translates dull and colorless speech into words with punch which will be remembered. In short, eloquence is where poetry and prose meet, where music and speech join. The means by which this is accomplished is by the adroit use of figures of speech, generally referred to as rhetorical devices.

TAKING SHORTCUTS TO ELOQUENCE

The title of this chapter is my version of what are normally referred to as rhetorical devices. I do so for the simple reason that, adroitly employed, these techniques allow novices to appear as very experienced speakers in the perception of the audience. Inexperienced speakers can learn to incorporate into their presentations techniques that provide polish to what may be an otherwise pedantic effort. Below are five of these shortcuts that will let you implant your ideas into the collective mind of your audience.

SHORTCUT ONE: REPETITION

Perhaps the most frequently used of these techniques is repetition of key words and key phrases to emphasize the presenter's message. An illustrative example is the famous 1963 speech by Dr. Martin Luther King, Jr. known as the "I Have A Dream" speech because he opened eight consecutive paragraphs with that phrase. Unless you believe you possess the oratorical skills of Dr. King, I would refrain from going that far in a business presentation. But a more limited repetition of key phrases does indeed add power to any presentation.

In a written essay such repetition would be redundant. In a spoken presentation it is an invaluable asset to hammer home the point you want your audience to grasp and act upon. Dr. King's speech shows how repetition can allow a presentation to build to a crescendo. Repetition is frequently used at the beginning of a presentation to gain the audience's attention.

SHORTCUT TWO: THE RHYTHMIC TRIPLE

One again I am coining my own phrase. The rhythmic triple technique, a variation of repetition, is generally called the Rule of Three, because it repeats, in threes, key words and phrases. I prefer the term, "Rhythmic Triple" because this technique delivers a message with an ear-pleasing rhythm and cadence in the beat of three.

The speaker using this technique drives home his or her point with three words, three sentences, three phrases. "Threes" tend to reinforce, because, for reasons no one fully understands, people remember best when they hear repetition in a series of three. Repeating twice is too few, four or more too much (unless you are a Dr. Martin Luther King, Jr.).

Sir Winston Churchill was a great user of the rhythmic triple. Here are two examples:

1. He praised the crews of Royal Air Force in the Battle of Britian, as they thwarted the efforts of the German Air Force, with this triple construction:

    "Never in the field of human conflict has so much been owed by so many to so few."

He could have said, "We owe a great debt to the fliers of the RAF in the saving of Britain." Would this phrase have been as memorable?

2. In the dark days of 1940, as Germany threatened to attack England, Curchill said in one of his most remarkable speeches:

    "I have nothing to offer you but blood, toil , sweat and tears."

Wait, you are saying, that's four, not three.

True. But in the retelling it is always "Blood, sweat and tears." Perhaps it is the redundancy of the words " toil" and "sweat," but it is also because the human mind has a template for "triples."

WHERE TO FIND EXAMPLES OF THE RHYTHMIC TRIPLE

Your local library will have copies of "Vital Speechesof the Day." Look for speeches made by prominent business and government leaders (written by talented speech writers). You'll find numerous examples of the rhythmic triple. You can then adapt these to your own requirements. You can also use a thesaurus or synonym finder to aid you in finding related words to link together in developing your rhythmic triple.

A word of caution. This is such a powerful device that employing it almost guarantees your point will be remembered by your audience. So be careful when employing it. Let's go way, way back to the 1988 Republican Convention. Then-Vice President Bush, against the advice of some of his economic advisers, used a double "Rhythmic Triple" in saying,

"Read my Lips: No new taxes."

Had he wanted to be vague, while still voicing his opposition to new taxes, he could have said,

"At this point in time, I assure you that I have no intention of engaging in any new revenue enhancing devices."

Those in the Convention audience, and Republicans watching on television, would have known he was promising to not raise taxes. The cumbersome phrase, however, would have lacked the cadence of what he actually said. He was elected President that year, of course, and then proceeded to raise taxes in 1990. During his bid for reelection in 1992 the Democratic Party kindly reminded the electorate of his double rhythmic triple. Had Mr. Bush not been so "eloquent" in 1988 he might have been reelected in 1992.

As with all these devices don't overdo it. You do not want to be so engrossed in "sounding" eloquent that you do not get your message across. Too many "triples" is similar to putting too much seasoning on food. It will take a lot of experimenting but once you are comfortable with this technique you have added a powerful weapon to your speaking arsenal.

SHORTCUT THREE: RHETORICAL QUESTION

This technique, where you pose a question and then provide the answer, can be used to draw an audience that may have "wandered off" back to the speaker's message. It can also be used to force the audience to reflect actively on what you have said, not just passively listen. You can also use it to lead into a summary of key points as well as a transition from one key point to another.

If you are making a presentation to a small group, and notice that a person is sleeping, you may wish to move close to that person, pose a question, wait about two seconds, and then provide the answer. The result will be an audience member who is now wide awake and very grateful that it was a rhetorical question, not one demanding an answer. Be cautious, however, in using this technique when presenting to a senior executive who might have dozed off. It will be more prudent to let others wake him or her up.

In drafting the presentation, look for places to insert rhetorical questions and then merely convert declarative sentences into question form. Voilà! You have automatically changed the cadence of your presentation. You also keep the audience attentive because they will not know if it is a rhetorical question or one where you expect someone to respond.

SHORTCUT FOUR: THE PAUSE

Inserted strategically, and occasionally dramatically, a pause is an effective means to call attention to a point just made, allowing the information to be absorbed before the next point is articulated. Developing the technique of the pause also forces a speaker who has a tendency to speak quickly to slow down. The pause can be effectively used to substitute for "uh" when you are reaching for just the right word.

Think of your presentation as vintage wine being poured into the small wine glasses of your audience's retention. You cannot pour constantly or else much of the wine will spill on the table. Stop pouring for about two seconds to permit another glass to be placed under the bottle.

SHORTCUT FIVE: CHIASMUS

Chiasmus, a term from ancient Greece, is the reversal of phrases within the sentence in the form of AB–BA. A very familiar use of this technique was in President John F. Kennedy's 1961 inaugural address when he said,

"Ask not what your country can do for you. Ask what you can do for your country."

Had he phrased this call to arms as a simple declarative sentence such as *"You should ask how you as citizens you can help your county in its time of need,"* it would have been far less effective.

There are a number of other rhetorical devices, but the ones provided in this chapter provide a solid start. Learn to integrate them into your presentations and meetings and you will be thought of as a very experienced and eloquent speaker, even if you are not yet at this stage.

In Chapter 18, we'll look at how to turn the often-dreaded Q & A session to your advantage.

CHAPTER 18

The Q&A Session: A Golden Opportunity

WHY IS IT that many people dread the Question-and-Answer session when it is so close to the conversational mode to which we are accustomed? Probably because they believe they are no longer in control of the agenda and that they run the risk of appearing less knowledgeable on the subject than they were in making the actual presentation.

The Q&A session should, however, be thought of by the well prepared speaker as an excellent opportunity to drive home points which he or she wants to emphasize to the audience. It is where you show to audience members that you can communicate as well on their turf as you can in your prepared presentation.

FEAR OF THE UNANTICIPATED QUESTION

I am repeating here much of what I said in Chapter 11 because it fits as well here as it did there. From my experience in training executives, diplomats, government workers, engineers, soldiers and lawyers, this particular fear has its root in the fear of being asked a question and not having the foggiest idea how to answer. Many presenters believe they must be able to answer all questions or they have failed. Absolutely not!

The simple solution when you don't know the answer is to say, "I don't know, but I'll get that information for you." Write the question down to demonstrate your sincerity. Make sure you do get the information to the questioner and, if feasible, to the entire group.

The best way to counter the fear of unanticipated questions is, as I said in Chapter 11, to make them anticipated by means of a thorough Murder Board. Engaging in this realistic simulation (Chapters 9 and 10) will enable you to anticipate many of the most likely questions your presentation will provoke. It will also cause your confidence to soar, somewhat like knowing the exam questions in college before an important test.

DRIVING HOME THE BOTTOM LINE

A great benefit of the Q&A session is that audience questions can provide the opportunity deliver a mini-presentation that focuses the audience's attention on those points the speaker wants understood and acted upon. Listen carefully for the nuance of the question, for some in an audience are inarticulate in asking their question. If necessary rephrase the question and inquire of the questioner if that is a fair summation.

While you are listening and repeating, be scanning your internal database to see what of your main points you can insert in the answer to reinforce your message.

As a general rule keep answers short so as to not enter into a dialogue with the questioner to the exclusion of the rest of the audience. By repeating the question you permit all in the audience to hear it, in addition to giving yourself the opportunity to be thinking of and refining your answer. A thoughtful pause before answering the question adds to your credibility.

NON-VERBAL COMMUNICATION

Maintain eye contact with the questioner at the outset of your answer. After about two sentences, look at other members of the audience. As you are ending your answer look again at the questioner.

While the question is being asked you should assume a relaxed position, with your elbows bent and your hands clasped lightly at waist level. Avoid folding your arms across your chest as that could suggest defensiveness or hostility to people who have read too many books on body language.

Be careful about nodding as you listen to the question. This is a habit we develop in conversations and it shows we are listening and tracking the question. If the questioner, however, suddenly takes on a critical tone at variance with the message you have delivered, continued affirmative nodding on your part could cause audience members to think you are now contradicting yourself.

PRIMING THE PUMP

When you say something like "I'd be delighted to answer any questions my presentation may have provoked," but no hands are raised, you may feel you have really bombed. Not necessarily so. Many people are reluctant to ask the first question after hearing a presentation because asking a question is, after all, "speaking in public." All the fears associated with this phobia affects audience members as well as presenters. Moreover, people realize they did not pay attention to every word spoken and are worried that their day-dreaming will be revealed if they ask a question about an issue which had been covered in detail during the presentation.

A way to get around this "no-questions" problem, one that I used in those infrequent times when I was greeted by silence, is to say, "A question I frequently receive is..." Then I posed a question, provided a succinct answer, then said, "Who has the next question?" This technique works most of the time. If, however, there are no questions, just say something along the line of "Well, I'm glad we are all on the same page and I thank you very much for giving me the time to discuss this issue."

DEALING WITH BELLIGERENT QUESTIONERS

When confronted with a belligerent questioner remain calm and certainly do not become embroiled in an argument. But at the same time you do not wish to be so conciliatory that you appear to have no convictions. You must stand your ground, using reason. If a questioner persists, a useful technique is to invite the person to discuss the issue with you after the presentation "because I am very interested in your point of view."

A questioner who asks a long-winded question might be hostile or might merely want to flaunt his/her knowledge to you and the rest of the audience. If you sense the audience is becoming irritated with the mini-presentation being given by a questioner, you must politely interrupt. While smiling, ask "Is there a question hidden in there somewhere?" If the questioner does not take the hint, interrupt more firmly, saying that there are many people in the audience who have questions and you wish to give them the opportunity to have their say.

BEWARE THE HIDDEN PREMISE

A variant of the belligerent questioner is the person who attempts to trap you by seeming to agree with your basic argument but in reality wants to trip you up. They may lead into the question with a phrase such as "Given the fact that..." followed by a negative interpretation of your position. When you see that the question has a hidden premise, challenge the questioner immediately, saying, "No, that is not what I said. Let me clarify and reemphasize my basic point."

AVOIDING A DIALOGUE

Because of the habits we develop in conversations of maintaining eye contact with the person to whom we are speaking, we run the risk of engaging in a dialogue with the questioner to the exclusion of other audience members. You want to include everyone in your answer. As you start answering the questioner, look at him or her for perhaps one or two sentences. Then look at another person, and then another. Come back to the questioner when you are completing your answer indicating that is the full answer. Break eye contact and look for another question. If you continue looking at the questioner, he or she may feel compelled to ask another question. You want to spread the questions around the room.

In Chapter 19, I'll show how to maximize the strengths of PowerPoint as well how to minimize its risks.

CHAPTER 19

Using, not Misusing, PowerPoint

AM NOT AN expert on PowerPoint nor do I wish to be. It is an excellent tool, far better than its predecessors--the 35mm slides and overhead transparencies. But its very strengths can be its very weaknesses. There are so many capabilities to the program that you may be tempted to use them all and cause the audience to suffer from what has been dubbed "Death by PowerPoint."

PowerPoint is relatively easy to use and has become a metaphor for graphics programs much as Xerox has become the generic word for photocopying documents.

Like all visuals, PowerPoint is an avenue into the brains of audience members that complements the presenter's intellectual message, body language and voice. Because we humans are primarily visual we need to see as well as hear.

There are exceptions. When I was facing critical audiences around the country while detailed to the State Department I never used visuals. To have used visuals in those situations would have opened me to the charge of being a "talking dog" sent out with a Washington-produced propaganda package. I had to "sell" myself before I could sell the policy and using visuals would have undercut my credibility.

So let's look at some experienced-based tips on using PowerPoint.

BE A MINIMALIST WITH "BELLS AND WHISTLES"

As mentioned above, do not succumb to the temptation to be theatrical. Just because you can have the bullet points do a double backflip, you don't have to do it. I have seen PowerPoint presentations which were a testimony to the ingenuity of the software developers at Microsoft--words appearing to fly off the screen toward the audience, vibrant colors I had never seen before and so on. The problem with these presentations is that I could not concentrate on the substantive content the presenter was attempting to convey, so impressed was I with the "pizzazz" of the slides bursting into my consciousness. I can remember all the "bells and whistles," but not the points the presenter was making.

BRING THE BULLETS ON ONE AT A TIME

Audience members can best receive the information if it is presented sequentially, not all at once. If you have, say, six bullet points, don'tbring them on the screen at the same time. While you are addressing point one, audience member may be wondering what you will say about the other points. My advice to my workshop participants is "Keep audience members' eyes and ears at the same place."

USE THE PROGRAM'S BUILT-IN COLOR SCHEME

Most presenters (including me) probably lack the skill of determining effective color coordination. I prefer the deep blue background, gold headlines, and white text. These colors coordinate well and are not distracting. Avoid mixing extreme colors such as fuchsia and orange. Keep in mind that approximately 8% of the American population has a degree of color blindness with regard to red and green. (Consider traffic lights.)

DOUBLE CHECK SPELLING AND GRAMMAR

Typos, grammatical errors, misspellings in living color on the screen are much more damaging than they would be in a memo. Don't rely on Spell Check (you've probably realized by now that it won't correct "there" to "their" or "it's" to "its") and don't rely on your own proof reading or that of your relatives, neighbors or friends.

CHOREOGRAPHY

Stand to the left of the screen (from the audience's perspective) because you are the principal visual and audiences read from left to right. They will look at you first, then at the visual on the screen. If you are on the right of the screen they will be distracted by looking at you, then back to the screen, then back at you.

AVOID READING FROM THE SCREEN

Face the audience and position yourself so you are not blocking the screen. Keep your feet pointed towards the audience. You can then turn slightly towards the screen with your upper body but if you do not make the pivot with your feet this position will be so uncomfortable that you will return to having eye contact with the audience, not the screen.

TALK FIRST, SHOW LATER

This is an unusual technique, but its novelty could pay off.

Explain the points you wish the audience to retain so members can develop an image in their mind. Then show the slide. The information is reinforced visually after you have caused the audience to think, not to merely receive the information passively.

Moving about in PowerPoint

Give audience members an occasional break by going to a blank screen. You don't have to turn the computer off. Just hit the B key and the screen goes blank. This is helpful when a discussion by audience members has veered from the information on the screen.

To return to a previously viewed slide, have a list of all slides by number. If you are asked to return to a slide, rather than backspace, refer to the paper, hit that slide's number, press Enter, and you are there. Use the same procedure to jump ahead.

The bottom line on PowerPoint

Let this outstanding program work for you but always keep in mind that, for serious audience members, content trumps pizzazz. As you are developing your presentation always remember that your job is to transfer information from you to audience members. PowerPoint can help you implant this information so these people will remember it, but excessive reliance on the "flashy" aspects of the program could result in your audience recalling how great your visuals were while being oblivious to your message.

Above all, remember that YOU are the messenger, and PowerPoint exists only to help you.

In Chapter 20, I'll show you how to end your presentation with impact by firing a "Final Arrow."

CHAPTER 20

Firing Your Final Arrow

ERHAPS THE MOST counter-intuitive aspect of my system is the concept of the Final Arrow. Employing this technique, when appropriate, can be among the most important elements of your presentation. Note that I said "when appropriate." You must know when to fire and when it is more prudent to keep that last arrow in your quiver.

Just what do I mean by the Final Arrow? Recall the discussion about the principle of Primacy and Recency, based on the empirical evidence that people tend to remember what they hear first and what they hear last, leading to the importance placed by trial lawyers on their opening statement and closing argument.

That of course, is the same reason I place so much emphasis on the 3–1–2 System of structuring the presentation so that the concluding words audience members hear--3--will contain the message that moves them to take the action desired by the speaker.

During the question and answer session the discussion may have ranged far and wide from the focus of the presentation. That is where the Final Arrow comes into play. it can have a profound impact on the success or failure of a presentation.

THE PRESENTATION QUIVER

Think of having a quiver of informational arrows on your back as you prepare to deliver your presentation. You fire your first volley to gain the attention of the audience in your Return On Investment (ROI) opening, flowing from the 1 of your structure. You show the audience you know their problem and you will be furnishing a solution.

Then you fire those arrows containing your supporting data: the 2 information which is the "meat" of your presentation. Finally, you launch the 3 arrow, driving home your point and probably setting the stage for questions from the audience. This is where focus can be lost. After you have answered questions from the audience, you might have an opportunity to fire the last arrow in your quiver: a distillation of the main point of your presentation--the point that causes the audience to take the action you have advocated.

KEY ELEMENTS OF THE FINAL ARROW

No new information

Because this element of the presentation will come after the formal close, it is imperative that you not introduce new information. This is the opportunity to <u>reiterate </u>and <u>reinforce</u> the main points of your presentation.

Deliver while doing "housekeeping" duties and in fifteen seconds

Audiences, say of senior executives, are not accustomed to hearing a speaker continue after being thanked for his or her presentation. They do realize, however, that notes must be gathered, laptops closed, etc. Fire your Final Arrow while accomplishing these tasks and maintaining eye contact with the key decision-maker. By doing this in fifteen seconds or less you come in under the radar, getting your main point across without alienating the audience.

When to hold your fire

If you sense an impatience among members of the audience and/or if you are running late, walk off with the arrow in the quiver.

In Chapter 21, our very last chapter, we'll discuss a vital but frequently ignored aspect of the presentation: The Post-Presentation Analysis.

CHAPTER 21

Post–Presentation Analysis

Almost as counter-intuitive as the Final Arrow is conducting a Post-Presentation Analysis. One's instinct, after completing what may have been an anxiety-filled, pressure-packed presentation, is to relax and perhaps enjoy a small celebration. Big mistake. Your senses are alert, your short-term memory in gear. You have just completed an intense, adrenaline-generating experience. If you are <u>never</u> going to make another presentation, then go celebrate and forget about all the lessons you have just learned, because you'll never need them. But that is the only reason you should avoid this "after-action" analysis.

Because you are reading this book I suspect you believe you will be delivering many presentations. One sure way to improve as a presenter is to learn from mistakes and then use these lessons learned as the springboard to better presentations in the future. The following are the steps to follow to achieve this constant improvement.

CONDUCT IMMEDIATELY

Short-term memory is precisely that. You must harvest the lessons of your just completed presentation within minutes, if at all possible, of completing the presentation. You'll soon forget the specificity of the give-and-take of the presentation, how audience members reacted to you, how you reacted to them, etc. If you wait even an hour, some particular memory or insight that could prove valuable for future presentations could disappear. Leave the site of the presentation for a relatively quiet place. With a notebook or, better yet, that handy audio recorder you used while practicing, retrace the presentation in your mind.

AUDIENCE QUESTIONS, OBJECTIONS, AND REACTIONS

What were the questions asked, the objections raised to the case you made? Note as well if any hackles were raised by points of your presentation. Who were the audience members most opposed to your position, and why were they opposed? Who were the people in the audience who sided with you? You can see where this analysis is going--straight to a data base for the next Murder Board. You'll find a similarity of questions raised and provoked by a presentation. Share this real-world information with your colleagues when participating in a Murder Board, making it more focused and realistic.

ASSESSMENT OF DELIVERY STYLE AND THEMATIC FOCUS

Now you can either pat yourself on the back or kick a little lower. Be frank in your self-assessment, but not overly critical. Look at this post-presentation analysis as an excellent opportunity to hone your skills in this vital area. Ask colleagues who were present for their frank opinions of what you did well, and where you need to improve. Include this assessment with your written and audio-recorded notes.

A FINAL WORD ON POST–PRESENTATION ANALYSIS

I will be redundant here. If you want to maximize the benefits of all the hard work you put into *planning, practicing* and *presenting,* you must conduct this analysis immediately after leaving the "stage." If you do not, you are doomed to reinvent the presentation wheel again and again. That will slow your progress toward excelling as a speaker. Isn't excelling as a speaker the reason you bought this book in the first place?

I sincerely hope this book, containing what I have learned in a lifetime of presenting, will help you improve your leadership skills by way of improving your persuasive ability. Please read the two articles in the Appendices to see how to implement what has been covered in these twenty-one chapters.

Good luck in all your presentations.

My Final Arrow

YOU ACQUIRED THIS book because you realized the quickest way to become an influential leader is developing your ability to speak persuasively. After reading these 21 chapters I hope you believe that the S3P3 System has provided you the tools to be such a leader.

What are the most important elements of this S3P3 System? Of all the words in this book, I believe the most salient center on drafting backwards with the "3-1-2 method," (Chapter 6) and practicing with the "Murder Board" (Chapters 9 and 10). The first provides you with focus and thematic unity, the next two allow you to anticipate objections and develop responses in advance. One from *Planning,* two from *Practicing,* all designed to make your *Presenting* more effective.

Famed motivational speaker Tony Robbins has said that persuasion is the most important skill you can develop. He's absolutely correct. Success in life depends on your ability to bring people to your point of view. But you can't just wish to be persuasive-you need a coherent, repeatable, system. That's what you acquired in this book. And remember: When you demonstrate your ability as a "public speaker," others will now think of you as highly intelligent and competent in all fields. This is the bonus known as the "Halo Effect."

Finally, a request. If you believe you can now "Bring Home the Bacon" as a result of learning the lessons in this book, I would appreciate it greatly if you could send a review to Amazon. "Indie" authors have a difficult time getting their books "discovered." When prospective readers see a large number of positive reviews, they are more likely to "Look inside" and hopefully hit the buy button.

Good luck on your road to influential leadership!

Larry Tracy

APPENDICES

Notes

Two Examples of how to Apply the S3P3 System:

Appendix 1
**Taming Hostile Audiences: Persuading Those
Who Would Rather Jeer Than Cheer**

Appendix 2
Model for a Winning Oral Presentation: The Philly Cheesesteak

I HAVE WRITTEN EXTENSIVELY on the art of presentation skills since becoming a speech coach. In preparing this book, I searched my files for articles which could best summarize and augment the lessons in "Bacon" by "pulling it all together." I wanted to show two distinct "types," so readers could see the versatility of the S3P3 System.

For Appendix 1, some context. I was a member of the Washington DC Chapter of the National Speakers Association (NSA-DC). Because the professional speakers in this group normally spoke to friendly audiences wanting to hear their message, they were not accustomed to speaking to resistant audiences. Consequently, I was asked, because of my experience, to provide lessons they could use if they were confronted by such an audience.

I taped my remarks, and NSA-DC sent the transcript to the prestigious magazine Vital Speeches of the Day, which published at the time only fourteen speeches per month of the thousands it received. "Taming" was published the following month. Then American Speaker, the leading publication on public speaking instruction, featured it the next month, with my photo on the cover.

In Appendix 2, I explain how I had an "Aha" moment when I concluded that the most famous sandwich in the US- The "Cheesesteak" from my native Philadelphia- is the perfect metaphor for the critical oral presentation which companies vying for a lucrative government contract often must deliver as part of the proposal process.

APPENDIX 1

Taming Hostile Audiences: Persuading Those Who Would Rather Jeer Than Cheer

Larry Tracy, Tracy Presentation Skills
Delivered to the Washington, D.C., Chapter of
the National Speakers Association, January 13, 2005

AM FREQUENTLY ASKED how I got into the field of presentations coaching after being a colonel in the U.S. Army. The first time that question was asked of me, my answer, I'm afraid, was a bit flippant. After reflection, however, I decided it was quite accurate. I said that early in my career I concluded, as did my superiors, I believe, that I could talk better than I could shoot. From that time on, I seemed to become the duty briefer no matter what my primary assignment. Ultimately I was selected to head the Pentagon's top briefing team, responsible for daily intelligence presentations to the Chairman of the Joint Chiefs of Staff and the Secretary of Defense.

My experience with hostile and difficult audiences came later when the White House assigned me to the Department of State for the specific task of speaking and debating controversial foreign policy issues throughout the United States and abroad.

Initially, I found it flattering that White Hose and State Department officials believed I was qualified to take on this task, but after the first few "confrontations," I realized these officials had decided it was better to place an Army colonel in jeopardy than a promising diplomat.

In all seriousness, however, that assignment was a wonderful life-changing experience. The almost 300 presentations, debates and panels in which I participated caused me to enter the field of speech training as my post-Army career. I knew that few people in this field had the real-world experience I had gained and could now pass on to others.

Let me say something that may offend some of you. Although you are all professional speakers, I submit that you are not a true professional if you are only capable of speaking to groups that agree with you.

The true professional speaker can deal with the jeers as well as the cheers. The true professional knows how to persuade the "non-persuadable," not just preach to the choir.

There is no greater challenge in the field of speaking than the task of bringing around to your position audience members who are initially opposed to what you are advocating.

Many people are inclined to take a fatalistic position at the prospect of dealing with such an audience. But that attitude is self-defeating. Bringing such an audience to your side by the lucidity of your reasoning, the coherence of your message, and the excellence of your presentation skills will indeed make you a complete speaker. As you have no doubt discovered, speakers in today's world must blend substantive mastery, focused structure and stylistic elegance to a degree not required previously. In today's contentious business and government climate, adversarial panels, debates, and presentations on controversial issues are more the rule, rather than the exception.

I want to divide today's presentation into two parts. In part one, I'll emphasize the importance of mastering the fundamentals of the speaking art. In part two, I'll show how to apply these fundamentals to persuading audiences inclined to disagree with you.

Part One: The Fundamentals of the Speaking Art

I know that some of you are thinking: "Hold on, we're professional speakers. We don't need any advice on 'fundamentals.' Just get to the good stuff — how to tame hostile audiences." Well, I disagree with those of you thinking that way. I have given over 3,000 presentations, and I always review the fundamentals. Let me use a sports analogy to emphasize this point.

By doing so, I am departing from the advice I teach in my workshops — "Men, go easy on the sports metaphors; you run the risk of alienating people in your audience who are not sports nuts." So please indulge me this one time, as the comparison is so apt. Professional football players are superb athletes who, in their games, employ complex formations, options and plays. Yet, when they report to training camp, they initially practice only football fundamentals — blocking, tackling, running, passing and catching. Only after honing these skills do these athletes move to their complex formations and plays.

Professional speakers should do no less. It is especially important when you are preparing to face a demanding audience. You may get by with a less-than-polished presentation when you are addressing people who agree with you, and only wish to have their views reinforced. It is, however, sheer folly to speak to an audience opposed to you without a strict adherence to the fundamentals of the speaking art.

Now, just what am I referring to with the word "fundamentals"? I don't just mean the platform skills of body language, eye contact, gestures and vocal inflection. They are indeed important tools for the speaker, but I mean something deeper. If your presentation does not take into consideration the objections, questions and other obstacles to understanding, it is unlikely the audience will accept and act upon your message.

Don't think of a presentation as merely a series of words strung together, any more than a bridge is merely wires and steel haphazardly connected. Just as there are sound engineering principles in bridge construction that take into consideration soil composition, prevailing winds, stress and strain, etc., there are sound principles which must be followed in the construction of a presentation.

Your mission as a speaker, to either a supportive or non-supportive audience, is to provide maximum information in minimum time in the clearest possible manner. Keep in mind that every presentation is actually four presentations: (1) the one you plan to deliver, (2) the one you actually deliver, (3) the one your audience hears you deliver, and (4) the one you wish you had delivered. I hope my presentation today will help you to deliver as you have planned and practiced, be on the same page as the audience, and have fewer of those "I wish I had said it this way" moments.

A motto of the National Speakers Association of a few years ago very elegantly described professional speakers as enjoying "The privilege of the platform." As a speaker, you have the rare opportunity to "write on the brains" of the people in your audience. Never undertake a presentation without that thought uppermost in your own mind. To communicate effectively and persuasively with any audience, you need "actionable intelligence" on these people. Note that I do not use the term "audience analysis," which is a favorite phrase of most of my colleagues in the field of presentations training. That phrase reminds me of high school students dissecting a frog.

When addressing an audience, you are dealing with living, breathing human beings with beliefs, attitudes, biases, prejudices, etc. Into that mix you will be adding new information. You must know their "what's in it for me" button, the pushing of which will cause them to listen to your message. You must know what problems these people have, so that your presentation can provide the information to solve these problems. This information must be delivered so it will be received by audience members. You must, in short, open the minds of these audience members.

So just how do you open the minds of an audience so your facts will be heard and accepted? You do so by going back to the teaching of history's greatest speech coach — Aristotle. He considered "ethos," which we would call "source credibility," the most important part of a speaker's means of persuasion.

He wrote in The Rhetoric, the seminal work on public speaking, that an audience which knew nothing of the subject being addressed would accept the position being advocated by the speaker if that person was considered to have "ethos."

Moving that Aristotelian precept to our times, we base our view on whether a speaker has credibility on three elements:

1. Expertise

2. Believability

3. Likeability

Your audience members want to know that you bring to the table information that will shorten their learning curve, that you have the credentials to speak on this issue, that you are telling the truth, not merely a glib speaker selling snake oil. Finally, they must like you. We all tend to accept information from people we like, and we reject it from people we do not like. Interpersonal skills are intimately connected to speaking skills. Credibility is subjective. No one in this room, including me, can say "I have credibility to speak on my specialty." Your audience members will decide if you are credible. If they do so, you are in a position to bring them to your point of view. If they do not, you are wasting your time speaking to them.

With all that in mind, I want to show you a systematic way of following the fundamentals of speaking. It is what I call the S3P3 system, the heart of my executive workshops. It worked for me in very challenging situations with resistant audiences and it works for my clients who, for the most part are not nearly as experienced in speaking as you are. Therefore, I know it will work for you. Let me ask you to open your mental PowerPoint, this time visualizing a pyramid supported by three pillars. The levels of the pyramid are, from the base to the apex, Planning, Practicing and Presenting. The pillars are Substance, Structure and Style.

Substance is the content of the presentation. Always remember that the purpose of a presentation is to convey information from speaker to audience members. Style refers to how you look, how you sound, your choice of words — all those attributes we ascribe to a good public speaker. Substance without style is a dry and boring recitation of data.

Style without substance is shallow and meaningless. Structure is the skeletal outline, or scaffolding, of the presentation. That's the word a young British Army lieutenant named Winston Churchill used in the title of a brilliant essay written in 1897, The Scaffolding of Rhetoric.

The future British Prime Minister emphasized that audience members needed a guide to show them where the speaker was taking them on this journey. A reading of Churchill's memorable World War II speeches, where it was said he "marched the English language into battle," demonstrates that he followed the advice he developed in his youth.

Such organization is vital for an oral presentation. A written memo can have faulty structure, but can be re-read. There is no instant replay of the oral presentation. Some examples of this structure are problem-solution, cause and effect, chronological. The presentation must have a beginning, a middle and an end. It must also have transitions which send signals to the audience that new elements will be discussed.

Now, let's look at that pyramid, starting with that wide base.

In Planning, you must develop a concrete objective, aimed at intersecting with the problems, needs, wants and concerns of your audience. This is always important but especially so when facing a demanding audience. Know specifically what you wish to have this audience do with the information you are providing. It is here where you draft your presentation, and this can best be done, in my opinion, by following my 3-1-2 System. While this system is counterintuitive, it virtually guarantees that you will have both focus and theme, vital for an oral presentation.

Take a stack of 3x5 cards. Mark one with a "3," and place on it the "bottom line" message you wish to impart to your audience. In front of these words, put "In summary," "In conclusion," or some other phrase signaling the end of your presentation. You now have your conclusion, as well as a mini-presentation, especially beneficial when making a business or sales presentation when time for the presentation is reduced at the last minute.

Take another card, mark it with "1," and use it to tell the audience where you are taking them on this oratorical journey. Next, place the supporting points that flow from "1" to "3" on a series of cards marked "2A," "2B," "2C," etc.

Using the 3-1-2 System will enable you to present maximum relevant content within the limited amount of time your audience may have to listen to you. You'll have more focus, because you will know when you start drafting where you are going with the presentation. Most importantly, audience members will see a structure to your presentation, enabling them to follow and, in the best of cases, ultimately agree with your argument.

Just remember: You draft 3-1-2, but when you have the allotted time, you deliver 1-2-3.

Now to Practicing, something many of us find rather odious. It is, however, vitally important, especially when preparing to face a difficult audience. Thorough practice will permit you to hone your presentation skills, anticipate questions, and it will certainly build your confidence. I teach my clients a three-step practice process. First, practice by yourself with a tape recorder and, if possible, a video camera. You are at your weakest at this stage and do not want anyone criticizing your performance. Listen for your "Uhs" and "Y'knows." The less of those abominations you utter, the less you will irritate your audience. Men, listen for a droning monotone. Ladies, listen for a high pitch.

Next, ask a colleague to be your "audience." This should be a person who can offer constructive criticism and comments. The third stage is to convene a "Murder board," a realistic simulation with colleagues role-playing your prospective audience. I'll cover this in more detail in just a few minutes when we focus on communicating with a demanding audience.

Finally, you reach that apex, Presenting. This is when you put voice to thought within a structure that facilitates audience comprehension and agreement with the position you are advocating, done with the style most appropriate to make your presentation memorable and successful. Eye contact, purposeful gestures, pleasant vocal inflection, skillful answering of questions are all part of the presentation. If you have practiced well, you will present well. For those of us who deliver similar presentations over and over, the challenge is to keep your material fresh. To do so, take a tip from the theater. Actors who play the same role night after night refer to this as "creating the illusion of the first time." As speakers, you can add new material, you can concentrate on getting yourself "pumped." Your obligation is to not be boring to members of your audience who are hearing your words for the first time.

Part Two: Persuading Hostile Audiences

Now let's see how we can apply these fundamentals to communicate with, and perhaps persuade, people who are adamantly opposed to our position. We live in an increasingly high-tempo, fast-moving, information-laden, real-time age, and the pace is picking up. Audiences are knowledgeable, critical, impatient, and demanding. Public debates and panels on controversial issues are becoming common. Perhaps it has been the institutionalization of presidential and other political debates over the last several years that has led to this state of affairs. Perhaps there is a "Super Bowl" desire deep in our national psyche that craves the clash of ideas, issues and rivals.

A debate or confrontational panel means sharing the platform with a person or persons opposed to you, perhaps with an audience acting as cheerleader for your opponent(s). You will then know how the Christians in the Roman Coliseum felt as they looked at the hungry lions. To be an effective presenter under such circumstances, a flexible "blueprint" must be developed for transferring information and perceptions from the speaker's mind to the minds of audience members.

When facing a skeptical or hostile audience, you must keep in mind that the information you are presenting is probably at variance with the preconceived opinions and biases of audience members. Anticipating how audience members will react, and what lines of attack any opponent(s) will follow, is an absolute necessity. Knowing your vulnerabilities, and developing responses/counterattacks, will enable you to snatch victory from the jaws of defeat, if I may use an overdone cliché.

I'll illustrate how failure to develop an effective counterattack had profound consequences for one of our political leaders several years ago. To make this interesting, I'd like to make a wager with you that in a few minutes, as I recount this story, some of you will be able to repeat, almost verbatim, something you saw and heard on television about 16 years ago. Any takers?

I didn't think there would be.

Let me tighten the focus. It's a cool October evening in 1988, and two senators are in the vice presidential debate. They are Lloyd Bentsen and Dan Quayle. I'm starting to see some knowing nods. I told you you'd remember. Quayle had been a controversial choice to be on the Republican ticket, due to his relative youth. To counter this perception, his campaign compared his age, and his time in Congress, to that of the late President John F. Kennedy.

In his memoirs, Quayle says that his "handlers," as he derisively referred to his debate prep team, feared Bentsen would turn the tables and make an unfavorable comparison of Quayle to Kennedy. They advised him to avoid any mention of Kennedy so Bentsen would not have an opportunity to skewer him. This was foolish advice, because in a debate one has no control over the questions. Quayle attempted to avoid the Kennedy comparison, but eventually, in response to a reporter's question, said he was the same age as Kennedy was in 1960, and had served the same number of years in the Congress as had the late president.

Now I see a lot of knowing smiles, and I would venture more than half of you know what happened next. Senator Bentsen said — and repeat after me — "Senator, I knew Jack Kennedy. Jack Kennedy was a friend of mine. Senator, you are no Jack Kennedy." What was Quayle's response? "That was uncalled for."

The remark by Bentsen, and Quayle's stunned reaction, was the most devastating and best-remembered exchange in the history of American political debates. Dan Quayle's image was permanently damaged, even though the Bush-Quayle ticket went on to win the November 1988 election. The Bentsen-Quayle debate provides an excellent lesson for all presenters. You must seek to anticipate the most daunting objections and questions your audience will raise. Failure to do so could result in public humiliation, the fate suffered by then-Senator Quayle.

Despite the fact that Quayle was, by all accounts, an effective Vice President, he never recovered from the Bentsen broadside. His every gaffe of the next four years was exaggerated by the media and TV comedians because it fit the image of the youthful, bumbling politician established in the debate. Could Quayle have neutralized Bentsen's broadside? Yes, with an intensive "Murder board," which I've mentioned in passing and will discuss in a few minutes. Had Quayle and his advisers decided to act on their worst fears, rather than put their heads in the sand and hope for the best, think how effective this response to Bentsen would have been:

"Senator, if you want to say who is not a John F. Kennedy, I would suggest you look at your running mate. The only thing Governor Dukakis and J.F.K. have in common is the state of Massachusetts."

Such a response would have taken little imagination to devise. A lemon could have been turned into lemonade by luring Bentsen into an "ambush," as a means of guaranteeing a hit on Dukakis.

Quayle's risk-averse coaches, however, took the cautious approach, hoping to deny Bentsen the chance to launch the attack they feared. Quayle and the Republican Party were ill-served by such incompetence. If Quayle had delivered such a response, his supporters in the audience would have responded with robust applause, Bentsen's comment would not have captured the headlines, and Quayle would have been credited with a quick-thinking comeback. The exchange would probably have been forgotten, and Quayle, who did well in the rest of the debate, would have possibly been viewed as the winner, or at worst the debate would have been judged a draw. Instead, he was considered the clear loser.

Now let's move away from history and back to today. A presenter can connect with even a skeptical audience by showing that he or she shares certain views with members of the audience. You must develop rapport and seek to establish common ground with the audience. If you don't, there is no chance of success in bringing these people to your side. You simply must, at the outset, open the minds of audience members.

Let me illustrate once again with a visual image. Imagine a car that is out of gas at Point A. This is your prospective audience, which lacks the vital information you will be imparting. You wish to drive this car to Point B — acceptance of your information. If the gas cap — the minds of audience members — is closed, any "gas" you pour will wind up on the ground. So how do you get that "gas cap" open?

You can do so by getting audience members to like or respect you. You can establish personal contact, perhaps by phone, with key members of the audience well before the presentation. In doing so, you'll not only establish that needed "human connection," you'll also gain additional intelligence on why these people are opposed to you. Arrive early so you can have conversations with people who are opposed to you. Learn more about their concerns, and why they are opposed to the position you are advocating. Perhaps you will learn who will be the troublemakers. You can speak with them in a non-confrontational way.

These people, in turn, may now see you more as a human being, not a remote corporate figure. During the actual presentation, mention the names of the people with whom you have conferred. Nothing is so sweet to the human ear as the sound of his or her name, especially if it is mentioned positively before others. These people that you mention will probably be less inclined to ask tough questions, as it could appear less than gracious after your kind remarks.

Next, find the necessary common ground by emphasizing areas where you and the audience agree, even at a high level of abstraction. This at least puts you and the audience on the same page, even if it is a small page. After establishing that there are points of agreement, you can then move to the arguments supporting your position.

A technique I used in facing audiences initially opposed to the position I was advocating was to acknowledge that we in Washington had done a poor job of articulating our policy, and I could therefore understand why so many people in the audience were opposed to this policy.

I would then say I hoped to fill in some of those gaps with my presentation. In this way, I was providing audience members with the opportunity to "save face," perhaps even to be willing to change their minds as a result of new information I was about to present. Remember that people don't want to admit they were wrong, and you cannot persuade people to change their minds: they must persuade themselves.

Now, let's look at three tactics for dealing with demanding audiences.

First, the "Murder board": The term Murder board comes from military briefings. It is a rigorous practice, a simulation of the actual presentation to be made. It consists of colleagues role-playing the actual audience, asking the type of questions this audience is likely to ask. As its rather macabre name implies, the Murder board is intended to be more difficult and demanding than the actual presentation. In football terms, it is a full-pads scrimmage. This realistic practice session is the most effective short-cut to speaking excellence. It allows you to make your mistakes when they don't count. It allows you to be exposed to tough questions, leading to focused research which enables you to provide succinct, accurate answers in the actual presentation.

In sum, the Murder board increases the odds that you will shine. When faced with the audience inclined more to jeer than cheer, it is essential to have such rigorous preparation unless you take some perverse joy in public humiliation. Next, stay within your evidence: During the give-and-take of a presentation with a demanding audience, you may be tempted to go beyond the hard, factual evidence that is the underpinning of your argument. An analogy or metaphor may be stretched beyond its limits, or a conclusion stated that is simply not supported by the facts. This can destroy your credibility, and provide a lucrative target for those strongly opposed to you. Credibility lost is difficult to regain.

Finally, you simply must maintain your composure in the face of hostility: It is quite natural to let your emotions take over if a person in the audience starts to harangue you. Natural, but a recipe for disaster if you lose your temper. Audiences will adopt an "us against the speaker" attitude if you respond in kind to a heckler or a person making obnoxious remarks.

I'll illustrate with an example from my own speaking experience when I was called a liar by an audience member. I was on a panel at a major university, addressing U.S. Latin American policy. The other three members of the panel were professors from the university, all opposed to that policy. The audience was composed primarily of students who, in the Q&A session, were aggressive but fair. Then a man in his forties rose and asked a "question" to which I responded. This was followed by two loud personal attacks against my honesty. I felt my Irish temper starting to boil. My instinct was to lash back.

Fortunately, for reasons I still don't understand, I did not. I said "Look, everybody in this auditorium wants to give me a hard time, and I can't just let you have all the fun." I broke eye contact, but he kept on shouting. At that point, another person shouted at the questioner: "Will you sit down and shut up? We want to get at him too." That struck me as funny — perhaps I have a perverted sense of humor — and I laughed. The audience joined in, and even my adversaries on the panel laughed. We then had a civil discussion of policy issues.

What would have happened if I had succumbed to the temptation of responding sharply to this man's accusations? The audience would have sided with him, I would have been booed, and the evening would have been quite unpleasant. The moral of this story? Keep your cool, no matter how provoked you may be. Your audience will respect you, and may turn on the heckler who is taking up their time. I fortuitously learned a valuable lesson that day.

Let me make some final observations about our profession. Emotions do indeed play an important role with any audience, but it is still verifiable, factual data that persuades reasonable people to come to your side. Above all, remember that you cannot persuade an audience; audience members must persuade themselves. Never tell them that you are going to persuade, sell or convince them. Do so and you are dead in the water. Allow audience members to "save face" by providing backing for your position with oral footnotes, and with information they did not have prior to listening to you.

Remember to maintain your composure, avoid personal attacks, and always keep in mind what you want your audience to do as a result of listening to your argument. I think a fitting way to conclude may be with one of my favorite quotations about the true purpose of speaking to any group. It comes from the birthplace of speech training and the art of persuasion — ancient Greece. The people of Athens, although admiring the speaker with the stentorian voice, dramatic gesture and clever turn of phrase, nevertheless realized the purpose of any presentation was to cause audience members to take the action the speaker wished them to take. So it was said, in comparing the greatest speaker of the day with one who had lived many years before:

"When Demosthenes speaks, people say 'How well he speaks.' But when Pericles spoke, people said, 'Let us march.'"

Thank you, and good luck in all your speaking ventures, to friend and foe alike.

APPENDIX 2

Model For A Winning Oral Presentation: The Philly Cheesesteak

By Larry Tracy Tracy Presentation Skills
(As published in the Newsletter of the Project Management Institute of Washington DC, May 2014)

YOU MAY BE assuming from the title of this article that it is a parody, a satire on the "How to be a Better Public Speaker" genre of self-help articles.

Not so. It is neither parody nor satire. Nor is it derivative classroom theory. It is It is based particularly on the knowledge gained in conducting scores of training programs for Project Managers and their teams of technical experts preparing to deliver oral presentations for lucrative federal government contracts.

This article had its genesis in a visit to my home town of Philadelphia. My coaching is based on a methodology I developed in my Army career where I frequently I gave presentations at high levels of government, and, at direction of the White House, debated controversial policies throughout the country, often to hostile audiences. I called the method the S3P3 System, the pillars of Substance, Structure and Style supporting a pyramid of Planning, Practicing and Presenting.

A key part of that methodology is counter intuitive. Drafting backwards in a 3-1-2 manner-Conclusion (3), Opening (1) and Body (2). Drafting any presentation this way increases focus, thematic unity and facilitates staying within the allotted time (Critical in an oral presentation for a government contract.)

Beneficial as it is, it remains counter intuitive, for we have been taught since elementary school to draft 1-2-3. So I am always looking for a way to explain this method inn ways my workshop participants can appreciate and adopt as their way of drafting, particularly as they prepard to deliver what theey hoped would be a contrct-winnning oral presentation.

During that visit to Philadelphia, I stopped by my favorite Cheesesteak place (In order to not alienate half of the City of Brotherly Love, I will not mention which one. As many readers probably know, Philadelphians are divided between Pat's and Gino's.) While savoring my cheesesteak, I had an "aha" moment. The perfect metaphor for a winning presentation was on a plate before me! The Cheesesteak could be he model for a contract-winning presentation.

Thinking this through, I came to the conclusion: The Oral Presentation-Cheesesteak comparison is based on their three similar components:

For the orals, 1) The opening statement by the Project Manager (PM), 2) The Technical Solution to the requirements of the RFP by the key personnel who will be working on the contract, and 3) The closing statement by the PM emphasizing the discriminators which make this the best company to solve the government agency's problem.

For the Cheesesteak, 1) The bottom half of the roll, 2) The steak, cheese and onions which are the essence of the sandwich, and 3) The top half of the roll.

Although I will be touting the importance of the PM's opening and closing statements, and the unique quality of the rolls of a Philly Cheesesteak, the most important elements are, of course, the middle two-the technical solution by the key personnel, and the ingredients of the sandwich. They are literally the "meat" which will cause evaluators to award, and eaters to salivate.

No one would buy a Cheesesteak that had no steak and cheese, just as no government agency would award a contract to a company whose oral presentation lacked a technical solution. But the rolls of the Cheesesteak, and the corresponding opening and closing statements of the orals, provide the context to decide which is a "winner."

Let's start with the orals. After all the submitted proposals have been reviewed by the government agency, they are whittled down to a precious few-those that are in what the government calls "The Competitive Range." There is not a lot of difference, or true discriminators, among these finalists. The companies all have similar technical capabilities to solve the government's requirements as specified in the Request for Proposal (RFP). Competing companies, therefore, must find a way to separate themselves from their competitors. The orals provide such an opportunity. Constructing an oral presentation the way a Cheesesteak is built can literally bring in the dough (Sorry).

Just as the technical proposals submitted to the government in response to an RFP can be virtually indistinguishable, the same is true for the ingredients for a Cheesesteak. So what separates the Philly version from poor imitations, such as the so-called "Steak and Cheese?" Ask Philadelphians, and they will exclaim "It's the Bread!"

The bread for Philly's contribution to culinary art are actually two rolls, which have a taste and texture unlike any other. It blends with, and complements, the Cheesesteak's cheese, steak and onions, for unequalled flavor. Displaced Philadelphians, when asked what they think of local sandwiches which claim to be Cheesesteaks, and they will sneeringly say, "ugh, the bread is terrible!"

UNLESS, that is, the bread is a Hearth-baked roll from Amoroso's, the Philadelphia bakery which now exports its product to all fifty states and the District of Columbia. A true Cheesesteak connoisseur knows the difference between crisp Amoroso's rolls and doughy imitations.

While you are probably salivating for a taste of Philly's finest food, let me now show how the "Amoroso's Factor" can provide a model for oral presentations, and what evaluators are looking for when they size up which company will get the "bread" from a lucrative contract. (Again, I'm sorry, just couldn't resist).

In the age of Low Price, Technically Acceptable (LPTA), there is little wiggle room on price. That leaves the Technical Volume as the area where there is some space to maneuver in order to increase the perception of "acceptability." When an oral presentation is required, the advantage grows, for the personalities and likeability of the presenters, and their ability to tell a persuasive story, can influence the evaluators.

Applying the "Amoroso's Factor" of a strong opening (the bottom half of the roll) and a resounding close (the top half)can be the deciding factor in causing the evaluators to award the contract to your company.

So what do these two "rolls" consist of in an orals? The main ingredient is passion and enthusiasm, thereby creating the perception that this company really wants the contract because it has the best capability to satisfy the government's needs. The opening (the bottom roll) should emphasize 1) past performance on similar projects, 2) the elements which separate this company from competitors, and 3) the credentials of the technical experts who will follow. The closing (the top roll) must drive home those same points.

The PM should deliver these book end opening and closing statement with an intensity that shows his/her confidence that the company is ideally suited for the challenges outlined in the RFP. That leads us the question of what these evaluators are looking for. They are certainly seeking the company which provides the best value for the government at the lowest cost. But they are also highly risk-averse and fear making a choice which results in being labeled "the idiots who gave the contract to that company." So these evaluators are between the proverbial rock and the hard place. What can you do to give your company an edge? You must first reduce the fears and perceived risk of these evaluators. Perhaps the greatest advantage of an oral presentation, for the government and the competing firms, is that it gives the government agency evaluators the chance to "size up" the people they will be working with for the duration of the contract. At the end of the workday, do they want to have a beer with these contractors, or be glad they can walk away from them?

In my writings and coaching teams how to conduct winning oral presentations, I list six elements evaluators are looking for:

- What is the chemistry between and among team members?

- Does the team have a clear vision of what the Government wants accomplished, or does the presentation suggest the team is still trying to figure out what is required?

- Do the skills of the different companies and individuals complement or clash?

- Is the prime contractor really in charge, or do there appear to be some Prima Donnas among the sub-contractors, suggesting later friction?

- Does the presentation demonstrate that the company has the experience to accomplish the project required by the RFP?

- Is there a willingness of team members to accept Government oversight, or an attitude of "give us the contract, then get out of the way?"

Keeping those six evaluator concerns in mind, let's construct an oral presentation using the "Cheesesteak" model. Just as the foundation of the sandwich is the bottom roll, the foundation of the orals is that opening statement by the PM. He or she, at the outset, must alleviate the worries of those risk-averse evaluators and create a positive perception of the company.

Here we apply the "3-1-2" method of my S3P3 System. Draft your Closing statement (the top roll) first, just as a trial lawyer would, and then set it aside for the moment. Then draft your Opening, just as the trial lawyer would to make his/her case to a jury. In the oral presentation, the PM makes the case why this company provides best value for the government, hoping to calm the nerves of the evaluators thereby convincing them they need not fear selecting this company.

The opening should signal the company's adaptability, showing it will keep the headlights on to see potholes in the road, and also be looking in the rearview mirror to see how actions could be improved. The PM must emphasize his/her past performance managing similar projects, and then introduce the key personnel who will be working on the contract, emphasizing their experience on similar projects.

It is these technical experts who are the "steak, cheese and onions" of the proposal. They specify how they will address the requirements of the RFP. showing how they can be innovative. The government likes that word because it can be interpreted as "at no charge."

Each technical expert should "hand off" smoothly to the next expert, demonstrating, they are a well-coordinated team. A competent presentation suggests a team that can work together without friction on the contract. Conversely, an uncoordinated presentation may be the kiss of death. After all, if a team cannot make a coherent presentation, how can it carry out a complex contract?

The top roll of the "sandwich" is, of course, the closing statement by the PM, reiterating those discriminators touted in the Opening. The PM's job is to cause the evaluators to conclude that this is the company which should be awarded the contract. These closing remarks need not be lengthy, and in fact should build on what was promised in the opening, much as a lawyer drives home the promises made at the outset to the jury.

A key element of an oral presentation for a government contract is that the government has mandated that oral presentation must be given by the people who will work the contract, not professional speakers or marketing specialists. These technical experts are very good at what they do, but not necessarily good at explaining what they do. Moreover, they are now being placed in the unenviable position of having the company's financial future-as well as their jobs, and those of their colleagues-dependent on their ability to make a "sales presentation."

Consequently, when I conduct orals coaching, I volunteer to draft both "rolls." As a technical illiterate, I rarely understand the details of the written proposal and the technical solutions by the subject matter experts in the orals. But as a writer, I can generally craft the story of why this company will give the government more bang for the buck.

I write these opening and closing statements in the "voice" of the PM so he or she can make these words his/her own. We then practice so the PM is comfortable delivering these messages. I also seek to find words or phrases which will "stick" in the minds of the evaluators. (Note: Read the excellent book Made to Stick by Chip and Dan Heath for some ideas on making ideas "sticky.")

An example. An IT company I recently worked with had an enviable record of low turnover of its key technical personnel, an important discriminator in the highly fluid IT industry. I learned that a reason for this stability was that when these experts published in professional journals, the company paid them a bonus. I then recommended the PM say the following:

In academia, the saying is "publish or perish." In our company the saying is "publish and profit."

The objective was not to turn a clever phrase, but to highlight the fact that the government would not be dealing constantly with new people, but would have continuity with the key personnel of this company. That's a huge discriminator, and that phrase helped the fact to "stick" in the minds of the evaluators, and be awarded the contract.

Continuing the Cheesesteak comparison, think of these rhetorical add-ons as the green peppers on a Philly Cheesesteak - they enhance the "flavor" of the presentation.

The next step, after "the sandwich" has been prepared, is to have a series of practice sessions simulating both the oral presentation and the Q&A session . These sessions should be videotaped to provide a "game film," and the proposal writers should play the role of the evaluators to help the presenters anticipate questions and develop answers. These simulated presentations and Q&A sessions are the "Murder Boards" of my S3P3 System.

A cautionary warning on the Q&A session. Because it is inter-active, unlike the orals where the evaluators sit silently, the PM and his/her team may relax. Big mistake - it is still "show time." Answer the question, but don't be overly verbose. The more you say, the more targets you provide the evaluators. When a question is asked that you find less than brilliant, don't say "Yes, but…." The evaluator who asked the question may feel you are putting him/her down. Instead, say "Yes, and we thought the same until our research indicated…."

For the same reason, avoid that terrible response of "With all due respect...". No respect is intended, and you will alienate the questioner. Just delete that phrase from your vocabulary for all presentations and conversations.

The benefit of intense and realistic practice session was shown in a Lockheed TV commercial of a few years ago. Two fighter jets were shown maneuvering in simulated combat, and a dramatic voice intoned "if you train the way you'll fight, you'll fight the way you trained". If presenters practice the way they'll present, they'll present the way they practiced.

Pointing out the importance of technical experts to be able to articulate their concepts, Lee Iacocca, former CEO of Ford and Chrysler, wrote in his 1984 autobiography:

"I've known a lot of engineers with terrific ideas who had trouble explaining them to others. It's always a shame when a guy with great talent can't tell a board or committee what's in his head."

We can say the same thing about a PM and the orals team which is unable to persuade government evaluators to award their company the contract. Just as an authentic Philly Cheesesteak needs the hearth-baked Amoroso's rolls to highlight the sandwich's ingredients, so too does the technical oral presentation need the right opening and closing statements to separate a company from its competitors. If you ignore these humanizing elements, and depend only on IT and engineering expertise, you are likely leaving a lot of money on the table.

Acknowledgements

TO THOSE WHO HELPED ME
IN THE WRITING OF THIS BOOK:

A BOOK IS PRODUCT of many hands, and that is certainly true of "Bacon." I found the first three members of "my team" via Google, the fourth by serendipity.

Knowing the text had to be formatted before being uploaded, I was very fortunate to find Glenn Bontrager. Based in Montana, he is the founder of Sarco Press. Not only is he an expert formatter but he also became my mentor, patiently and kindly introducing me to the mysteries of self-publishing. Glenn can be reached at glenn@sarco-press.com It was Glenn who put me in touch with Kerry Jesperger, my talented cover designer. The cover of this book was her idea and she was very patient with my constant "tweaks." Kerry can be reached at kerry@aerogallerie.com

The luck of the Irish enabled me to discover Laurence O'Bryan, founder of Books Go Social in Dublin, Ireland (www.booksgosocial. com). Laurence and his team deploy social media to give self-publishers the worldwide exposure they could never achieve on their own. Additionally, Laurence hosts the annual Dublin Writers Conference which my wife and I attended in June 2018. Panels of experienced writers and publishers teach the trio of writing, publishing and marketing for both the traditionally-published and self-published authors. Laurence and his team have been constant sources of suppoort, always responding to my frantic email seeking advice.

Purely through good fortune did I discover my editor, Christie Wagner. My wife and I met her socially, and only after some time did I find out she was a world-class editor, ghost writer and author who had also worked in the Office Of Presidential Speech Writing at the White House. Christie can be reached at ChristieWagner@gmail.com.

Last, and certainly not least, is Amy Collins, CEO of Newshelves books, possibly the leading expert in the US on selling and marketing books. I met her at the Dublin Writers Conference, where she delivered the best presentation, and also gave me invaluable advice on self-publishing. She will be recommending this book to 1000 book stores in the US. No matter how good a book is, to be successful it must be discovered. Amy is the "Christopher Columbus" for self-published authors.

TO THE PEOPLE WHO ENABLED ME TO BECOME A SPEECH COACH

In my military career I had many opportunities-and a lot of luck-to develop my speaking skills. While I had given briefings at high levels as a Lieutenant and Captain in the US and Vietnam, it was an assignment as a Major to be the intelligence instructor at the U.S. Army Engineer School at Ft. Belvoir, Virginia outside Washington DC where the S3P3 System was really developed. I decided to eschew the standard Army instructional mode of lecturing, and conducted my classes in the highly participative manner that appeals to adults. Unfortunately, the Colonel for whom I worked was not pleased and ordered me to follow the Army method.

Then fate intervened in the person of the school's Commandant, the results-oriented then-Brigadier General Ira A. Hunt. Because my courses were receiving the highest ratings from the students, he told the conventionally-minded Colonel to back off, and allow me to teach those courses "my way." The General also "flew cover" on my performance reports so the rather angry Colonel could not ruin my career with a poor evaluation. I am eternally grateful to General Hunt for allowing me to develop the S3P3 System, and very appreciative of the gracious testimonal he wrote for this book.

A few years later I was assigned to the Defense Intelligence Agency (DIA). I was working as a Latin American analyst, and my boss, Colonel Leo Boucher, believed, after seeing me deliver a briefing, that I would best serve DIA by being the lead briefer. The Director, LTG Daniel Graham, then interviewed me for the position of Chief of the Presentations Branch.In this position I would be responsible for the daily briefing to the Chairman of the Joint Chiefs of Staff (CJCS). In offering this assignemnt General Graham told me I would become the best known Major in the Penatgon, but if I embarrased him or DIA, he would fire me immediately, and that would ruin my career. He then asked, without pausinng, "Do you want the job?" The only answer was "Yes Sir." It turned out be a fabolous learning experience. I am immensely grateful to both Colonel Boucher and the late LTG Graham.

In the almost three years I held that post, I was, as stated above, responsible for the daily intelligence briefing to the CJCS and his three-star staff. I headed a team of six outstanding briefers and facilitated over 500 of these multi-screen, multi-media presentations, personally presenting to the Chairman and his staff almost 100 times. We also had a steady stream of "customers"-key military and civilian officials in the Pentagon who wanted to receive the same briefings as the CJCS, as well as various Defense Department organizations throughout the Washington DC area. We also briefed Congressional staffs. In short, we were a busy bunch.

An added benefit of holding this postion was that I became the "mentoree" of the finest briefer in the Pentagon, the late John Hughes, senior civilian in DIA. He had developed a presentation titled "The Soviet Military Buildup: The Evidentiary Base." It was highly classified, primarily satellite photos of the rapidly expanding Soviet intercontinental ballistic missile program. This briefing became the hottest ticket in town for those with the highest security clearances. It lasted two hours with about 170 overhead slides in those pre-PowerPoint days. So fascinating was this briefing developed by Mr. Hughes that no one fell asleep.

He asked my two-star boss to let me learn and deliver the presentation when he was not available. I wound up delivering it 90 times in one year! Mr. Hughes and I met twice a week to go over questions asked by our respective audiences. These audiences included US Ambassadors in Washington for consultation, Ambassadors going to their posts, key officials of the Pentagon, members of Congress and their staff members-just about anybody with the requisite clearance. These twice-weekly meetings became tutorial sessions for me on the art of presenting, and the lessons I learned from Mr. Hughes have been the vital elements of the S3P3 System.

Some years later, the White House directed the Army to assign me to the State Department to debate controversial security issues throughout the country. Those three years I spent at State provided me experience unlike any I had previously. I participated in hundreds of debates and panels, the majority before contentious audiences opposed to US policy and with debate/panel adversaries supported by theses audiences. My State Department colleagues joked that I was "the guest of honor at public hangings." At colleges, I was frequently escorted on to the stage by campus security. I took it as a measure of success that it was never necessary to be escorted off the stage.

In summary, I owe much to the people who gave me the opportunities to develop my speaking skills and my S3P3 System. My career as a speech coach, and this book, would not have been possible without the confidence they placed in me.

For Further Reading
And Citations

Welch, Jack Interview, Published , February 2016

Lee Iacocca, Iacocca: An Autobiography, (Bantam Books, New York, 1984,) 58

Burning Glass Technologies, Study, April 2016

Raisel, Ethan M and Friga, Paul N The McKinsey Mind (McGraw-Hill, 2002), 107

Safire,William The Dictionary of Political Terms (Oxford University Press, 2008), 408

Wallechinsky, David, Wallace, Irving and Wallace, Amy The Book of Lists (Bantam Books, New York, 1977), 469.

Mehrabian,Albert, Silent Messages (Wadsworth Publis. Company, Belmont, CA., 1971,)140

Atkinson, Max Lend Me Your Ears: All You Need to Know About Presentations, (University Press, New York, 2004), 342, Atkinson, 345

Restak, RichardMD, The Brain (Bantam Books , New York 1984)

Kunkel, Vicki Instant Appeal: The Eight Primal Factors (AMACOM, New York, 2008), 416

Morgan, Nick, Power Cues (Harvard University Press, Cambridge, MA,2018), 78, 79, 171

Index

Made in the USA
Middletown, DE
10 May 2019